Into No Woman's Land

War Stories of a Female

Construction Worker

A Memoir

by Amy R Farrell

For ...
Edward Lawrence Farrell
and Joan "Jody" Oppermann Farrell,
who told their little girl she could grow up to
be whatever she wanted, but who never
dreamed she'd grow up to be
a construction worker.

...and for my brother Steve,
whose beautiful life was far too short.

Note to Reader

What follows is a recounting of my personal experiences, retold with due diligence as to its veracity. Conversations cannot be remembered word for word, nor events recalled with absolute accuracy, after the passing of decades.

In every case I have presented these "war stories" as I remember them. I have changed the names of companies I worked for and of persons I worked with. If I mention the place in which a given job took place, it is because the location is vital to the story. My reader will please forgive the almost-continuous use of foul language on the part of the construction workers in this book, including myself. A story about construction workers without flagrant cussing would stretch the bonds of believability. And the fact is, this is how we really talk on the job.

-Amy R Farrell, 2013

Amy R Farrell

PART ONE:

LABYRINTH

We have only to follow the thread of the hero path, and where we thought to find an abomination, we shall find a god. And where we had thought to slay another, we shall slay ourselves. Where we had thought to travel outward, we will come to the center of our own existence. And where we had thought to be alone, we will be with all the world.

-Joseph Campbell, The Power of Myth

Amy R Farrell

1

Following A Thread
In which I embark upon a strange journey

My 1979 Toyota truck bumped over the dirt road, raising a
cloud of powdery High Sierra dust while I turned the wheel, driving
with my plastic lidded travel-mug with the red and blue Chevron logo
clenched between my thighs. I came out into a clearing crowded with
beat-up vehicles and parked my baby-blue pickup in the last remaining
spot between two towering fir trees. I shut down the motor, drained the
last of the now-cold coffee and dropped the cup onto the floorboards.
Waiting for the cloud of dust to billow and dissipate past the dirt-
streaked window, I peered out at the men.

They stood around a small smoking fire made of 2x4 ends and
paper cement sacks, drinking coffee from battered Stanley thermos
bottles and puffing on Marlboros, talking. They were bundled up in
canvas and denim coats. Their Levis and Wranglers blue jeans were stiff
with grease and grime and their boots were half-buried in the powdery
soil. I took a deep breath and reached for the door handle. Getting out,
I grabbed my hard hat, gloves and lunch box and slammed the door.

It was May 17, 1986 and I was a young woman reporting for her first day of work on a construction job.

I approached, gloves in my back pocket and hard hat under my arm. I slipped into the circle of men, dropped my hat and lunch box at my feet and extended my fingers towards the fire. Glancing up, I looked at the men. Their faces were weather-beaten, their hands gripping cups rough and scaly, fingernails black and broken. "Who's the girl?" one of the men inquired of no one in particular.

"Flagger," said one of them, probably the foreman. He was a big man with dark hair and a thick beard that grew down his neck and disappeared into his shirt collar.

"Laborer's Union. Local 294," I proudly said, reaching in a pocket to touch my union card, ready to pull it out in case they wanted proof. The foreman spat tobacco juice into the fire with a sizzle. "That's all right," he said. "Darce Daniels called and told me he was sending you up the mountain." The men returned to their conversation regarding the job and who would go where on the site to do what and with what. They were all dirty and smelled like old sweat and last night's alcohol and I didn't understand a word they were saying. They talked of 245s and bobtails, D9s and transfers, belly-dumps and pull-boxes, wackers and vibro-plates, and I waited, my heart a bird beating its wings against bars.

The smoke from the fire swirled and rose in tiny devils, casting ashes into my eyes, making them water. My long blond hair was braided in a queue down my back and wisps of it had escaped and were fluttering against my cheek in the chilly breeze that blew up-canyon through the pines. I kept brushing it away, aware that it was a sure marker of my femaleness here in this all-male place. I put my hard hat on, hoping to corral it. The hat was an aluminum one with "U.S. Government" stamped on the brim, from my stint last summer as a six-dollar-an-hour emergency wild-land fire-fighter for the National Park Service. The yellow spray-paint was mostly worn off of it and it was sooty-looking. I hoped it gave me an air of having done this before. I hoped it might disguise my girlness.

An ugly bear of a man with brown teeth leered at me over the fire and poured the last of his coffee into it with a sizzle and a puff of steam. "I'll take the girl with me, boss," he said. "I got a little flaggin' she can do."

The foreman didn't even respond. "All right, guys, let's get to work!" he said and gestured me to follow him. He stuck big grubby hands into the pockets of his grease-streaked canvas coat.

"You're a little thing," he said as we walked to his truck. The steel was showing through the toes of his work boots. He pulled open the driver side door on the dusty white pickup. "What else can you do 'sides flag?" he asked.

"Anything," I said and hoped it was true. I had recently broken three ribs while shoeing a horse, an experience that had shaken my confidence about becoming a professional farrier, a wake-up call after successfully completing a twelve week course in farrier science at the Porterville Horseshoeing School. My ribs were only half-knitted, but hearing they were looking for flaggers at $18 an hour on "the Sierra Project," I had paid three hundred and twenty-five bucks (most of which was borrowed) to join the union, hoping to get one of the lucrative flagging jobs. I figured even busted up as I was, I could hold a stop/slow paddle and make some money while I figured out what my next career step would be. After being knocked down and trampled, I was scared to get under a strange horse again.

The foreman jutted his chin, indicating I should go around and get in the other side. I bounded around the front of the truck and jerked the right side door open. Pressing my hand against my side, I clambered up onto the cluttered bench seat, hoping the man won't notice I was in pain as I pulled myself up using the ceiling-mounted Jesus-handle. He didn't even glance at me as he put the key in the ignition. Shoving soda cans, crumpled KFC bags and empty mayonnaise-slimed sandwich baggies off onto the floor, I skooched in next to a battered briefcase and a clipboard loaded with trucking receipts. I held my lunch box in my lap and took a slow deep breath, waiting for the ache in my side to subside.

"Can you run a Rammax?" he said, starting the motor and putting the truck in gear.

"Sure," I said, wondering what the hell a Rammax was.

We drove on a dirt road through pristine forest, the sparkling green needles of pines and firs catching the early rays of the sun and the rich hues of browns, golds and grays blending into a palette that if I was painter I would love to dip my brush into. The forest floor was a tangle of pungent bear clover, twining white-thorn and here and there the bright red thrusting tip of a snow-flower emerging from duff. Moss-covered granite boulders were interspersed between the massive trunks of trees and I heard the caw of a raven that winged its way twixt the pines, its pinions whistling. The yellow sunlight filtering through foliage collecting into bands of brightness streaming towards my eyes cast the scene in high relief and I noticed fine details, the silvery gleam of facets of the sugar pine's bark, the multitude of insects busy on the air, the darting quickness of a chipmunk racing for cover.

Then diesel fumes overpowered the scent of cedar. A scene of destruction lay at the terminus of our winding road through beauty. The roar of machinery, dust clouds rising to the sky and the ear-breaking squeal of metal against metal as the tracks of a huge excavator ground against one another when the monster lumbered by. Trees were down in a broken mass, limbs and roots together being pushed into a heap by a big yellow bulldozer, along with dirt, rock and duff in a whirling, swirling, crushing display of power.

"I'm Skip," the foreman said. His big hand with its blackened fingernails scratched at his heavy beard. A speck of chewing tobacco sat on his lower lip beneath a mustache so long it curled over his upper lip into his mouth, wet with saliva. "I'm gonna start you here, in the trench-line. Ain't got no flaggin' right now, but you can run the Rammax." Skip opened the truck door and got out.

"Great!" I said, hoping I sounded confidant and capable. I slid out and fell into step beside him. Where we were headed, about twenty men were working, climbing up into the cabs of heavy equipment or jumping down into a deep trench or crawling on hands and knees dragging a cable around bundles of pipe and rebar.

"Ain't never had no girl on the job," Skip mentioned.

"Oh," I said, "yeah." The foreman's stride was long and I had to hop to keep up.

"How long you been in this?"

"A while," I lied. His head jerked around like pulled on a string. A suspicious brown eye lit on me but he kept walking. "Not in the union though," I amended. I knew he could easily check.

"Scab."

I kept my mouth shut. I knew what a scab was, had been taught in a high school social studies class about the labor movement in America. I didn't want to be a scab. Skip said nothing else about it.

The Rammax, as it turned out, was a machine for the compaction of soil in a trench. It was a big thing, about the size of a large chest freezer, painted orange, with "sheeps-foot" steel roller-drums and hand levers for control. At Skip's direction, I ran a chain through the ring on the top of the machine and attached the chain to the excavator's bucket. As I hooked the chain back on itself, I was already noticing the glares of some of the men around me. I heard one comment, delivered in a stage whisper clearly meant to reach my ears.

"She's got a lot of balls coming up here." Then a response.

"She'll need bigger balls to stay. Whatya bet she won't come back tomorrow?"

A short hard laugh. "Five bucks says she'll be outta here by noon."

I didn't understand the hostility. I didn't yet know that by coming here I was treading on a proving ground of manhood. The horseshoeing school had been one such proving ground and the men there had politely tolerated me and Sally, the other girl who had attended the 1985/86 Winter session. The horse world was full of women, however, as riders, breeders and trainers, if not yet as farriers. In contrast, the construction world was, in 1986, an unknown country for the female gender.

Another laugh. "Ten bucks says she and Skip'll be fucking in the office trailer by noon." Guffaws of laughter.

Skip squirted a stream of juice and shook his head, but he couldn't quite hide the smirk on his face. Before he walked away, he reached out and grabbed my shirt cuff in one strong hand. I looked up into eyes as indifferent as loneliness. He leaned in so close I could smell the minty scent of his chew and see the wet tobacco caught in his mustache hairs. "I am only trying you out," he said.

My temples were thrumming but I met his unbroken gaze. "Yes, sir," I said.

Skip let go of my cuff like he was throwing something away. His shoulders hunched against the seams of his canvas coat and he walked away like a man who had already fired me. I took a deep breath and turned to look at the excavator operator. He wore a blue-and-red checkered shirt so filthy it looked like old road-kill. I smiled at him and signaled that the chain was secure. There was no returning smile but the hydraulics whined and he lifted the Rammax up into the air and lowered it into the five-foot deep trench. I jumped down after it, steadied it as it was lowered, then unhooked the chain. The boom of the excavator swung it away, then stopped suddenly, causing the chain to bounce and whip back towards my face.

My hand raised instinctively, blocked the heavy steel hook from cracking into my nose and took a stinging blow across the knuckles. I glanced up at the operator, expecting to see surprise and contrition in his expression but there was only a stare deadpan as a poker player's, compassionless as a shark's. I had never known such a look. With a squeal of metal, the man rotated his monster machine and tracked away, leaving me with my knuckles slowly turning purple inside the leather work glove, next to the Rammax.

A dark-skinned old man with a shovel on his shoulder walked up the trench. "You run dis machine before?" he asked in a voice accented like strong tea. Soothing sweet tea. I started to speak, then stopped, wondering what I should say. There was something in his hazel eyes that stopped me from lying.

"Ah," he said, nodding. "It is like this," he said, and moved to the controls. He showed me how to start the Rammax, how to make it move forward and backward, how to adjust its direction using the tractor-brake theory (one side stops moving while the other side continues, creating drag on the one side which turns the machine) and how and when to engage the vibration feature.

"Thank you, *Señor*," I said when he was done showing me.

"I am Placido," he introduced himself. "I will help you if I can."

Against my wishes, my throat choked up. The old man reminded me suddenly of my father who had died three months before while I was at the horseshoeing school. Pop had paid for my tuition, pleased and proud that I had settled on a career that was artistic (because of the iron-working), scientific (because of the physiology), laborious (because he knew his daughter liked a physical challenge) and working with animals (which he knew was my great love). It was torment for me that he had not lived to see me graduate. The fact that I had now turned my back on the farrier career was another torment. And because I was scared. Me, scared of horses! Pop's brave scared-of-nothing no-quitter daughter.

I struggled against thoughts that if my father knew he would be so disappointed. Swallowing hard, I tried not to look directly into Placido's gentle eyes. His kindness, especially in contrast with the other men's enmity, gave me hope that I could, in fact, endure, if not succeed, here on the Sierra Project.

Come on, girl, I told myself, you've only just started, don't let it buck you off! I took off a glove and reached out my hand to the old man. He glanced down at the purpling place the chain had struck me. His lips pressed together. Warm rough fingertips squeezed mine gently and released, like one would touch a trembling horse. I smiled, recognizing the horseman in him. It was an instinctual thing that couldn't be taught, knowing just what was needed and when and not too much. As it was meant to, it calmed me.

"My name is Amy," I said to Placido. "I appreciate your help very much."

Amy R Farrell

2

Biscuit And Gravy
In which a rank horse makes hash of me

Mrs. Farley's fat, spoiled Appaloosa mare had not, the owner informed me, had her feet done since the last horseshoer had departed in disgust three years before, chucking his trimming tools into his tool box and racing his own shadow down the Farleys' long twisting driveway.

What was my first clue? I didn't heed it, thinking that what I had been told at Porterville by my teacher, Mr. Newmar, regarding the calming effects upon rank horses of a female farrier would serve to make this job a charm. Who better to soothe a nervous mare than me, a lover of animals all my life? Any creature of flesh and blood would see in me a kindred spirit, someone who would never do them harm, someone in whom to place their trust. Surely not someone who needed the shit stomped out of them.

Having completed my farrier course in February, I had hung my shingle in Three Rivers, the small central California town I lived in, hoping to become "the local horseshoer." Indeed, I did get calls. The fat

Appy mare of Mrs. Farley was the third horse of my professional career. She was a Leopard Appaloosa, white with black spots all over.

"She's very sweet really," I was told, as the mare pinned her spotted ears against her poll and drew wrinkled pink lips back baring long yellow teeth.

"Yes, she seems very nice," I said, dodging a lightning-fast nip.

Mrs. Farley gave a flick of the lead rope, more playful than admonishing. "Now, Biscuit, stop being like that," she purred at the big ugly horse. "Amy and you are going to be great pals. Just wait and see how good your feet feel when she's done with you."

I gathered up my hoof-knife, rasp and nippers, holding them out to the mare to examine. She stood impassively, not looking at the tools, not sniffing them. A bad sign. I wanted the horse to acknowledge me and what I was there for, to buy into what I was bringing, but I couldn't wait all day. I put the tools in my left hand and reached out to stroke the mare's shoulder with my right. She flinched at my touch and stamped a dinner-plate-sized hoof on the ground, splayed and ragged. Her threadbare tail slapped down between her fat buttocks.

"Easy there, Biscuit," I said, "quiet now." I stroked the horse until she stood without stamping and her tail lay quiet. I waited until I heard her exhale a long breath. Running my hand down from her shoulder to her knee and finally to her pastern, I gently squeezed the fetlock between my thumb and forefinger.

Biscuit picked up her foot. "See? She's really very good," Mrs. Farley said.

So far, I thought. Something had made the other horseshoer leave. Holding the foot loosely in my left hand, I used the unsharpened edge of the hoof-knife blade to scrape the packed mud and wedged gravel out of the mare's distended foot. A foul stench plucked at my sinuses as I dug black tar-like thrush out from between the rubbery frog and the thick grainy sole. I let Biscuit put her foot down to rest.

"Her feet are really overgrown," I said, taking a breather myself. Farriery is backbreaking work. It is the only job I know where you work in a crouch and use your knees as a vice to hold your medium. "Easy, girl," I said, as I picked up the foot again. This time I raised one leg and pulled Biscuit's hoof under it into my lap, clamping the horse's pastern firmly between my knees. The mare squirmed and tried to jerk her foot away, but I held on until she stood still.

"That's right, easy as pie," I said in an even tone. I began to cut the flaking sole and flapping frog away, paring it down to a neat clean normal equine hoof. Big hunks of reeking horse foot lay scattered around my boots as I gouged a track around the jagged hoof wall where I would soon lay the sharp blades of my nippers.

Mrs. Farley's blue Queensland Heeler, Blaze, darted in and grabbed a piece of foot and dashed away to bury her prize under a buckeye tree. I slid the knife into the pocket of my leather chaps and picked up the nippers. Squeezing the long polished handles together repeatedly and sliding the blades along, I cut the splayed edges of the hoof wall away, tossing a long curling piece to Blaze where she lay under the buckeye with dirt on her nose from using it as a shovel. The dog snapped it out of the air and began lustily to chew on it.

Nipping the last piece away, I shoved the hoof forward with my thumb, sighting down along its flat surface, checking for lateral balance. Satisfied, I exchanged the nippers for the rasp. Mrs. Farley chatted amiably as I worked, holding the lead rope loosely in her hand. Setting the foot down when I was done, I stood back and looked at it from several angles. "That's much better," I said.

"There, Biscuit, aren't you glad Amy came?" Mrs. Farley asked the mare. Biscuit didn't answer, just wrinkled her lips and looked at me from under hooded eyelids. I trimmed the other front foot to match. I stooped to gather up my tools and start on the hind feet. "Since you two are getting along so well," Mrs. Farley said, "I think I can go get ready for my tennis game."

I looked up from my tools and said, "I thought you'd be here to hold both the horses while I worked on them."

She gestured at the other horse, a mud-colored gelding tied to the fence. "Oh, he's no trouble. That's why we named him Gravy. It's Biscuit who's a handful, but you two are getting along like eggs and bacon!" She tied the mare's head to the corral and began the long walk up to the house.

The minute she disappeared within, and I was squatted under the Appy's fat rear end with a hind foot in my lap, the horse exploded. Not in the sense that a stick of dynamite within her intestines suddenly ignited, spewing guts and bloody body parts all over the place, but for me, no less surprisingly. She went straight up in the air, all four feet, including the one I was rasping, airborne and flailing wildly. I was spun around and went down under her, somehow ending up on my back, breathless, with my legs between her front feet and my head on the ground between her hind feet, looking up in startlement at her flabby teats.

The big horse was rearing and jerking her head against the halter rope, trying to free herself. When this failed, she began to pitch and buck, her hind hooves, with each jump, flashing past my face and mercifully landing on either side of my head. I tried to shimmy out from under the pitching beast but flying hooves were everywhere. As she pulled back against the rope she fishtailed back and forth and I was hard-pressed to keep from being stepped on. I decided to try to scoot myself backward and thus escape from her trampling ground. Scarcely had I begun upon this course, when she entered into another bucking fit. Up, down, up, down, went her hooves landing each time on the ground to one side or the other of me, then finally down she came, landing on my chest just below my left breast. Then she stood stock still, one foot and a great deal of her massed bulk upon my chest.

My rib cage was in a vice. I could feel my back against the hard ground of the paddock, every small pebble, little stick and grain of sand impressed into my skin. The hoof under my breast was the one I had but recently nipped and begun rasping with my horseshoeing tools, the edge was sharp as glass. I could feel it cut me, feel the blood trickle down my side. Meanwhile, the mare stood there, resting half her weight on me as if she didn't know what to do. Every once in a while she snorted and leaned back on her rope, putting more weight on me. I could feel my ribs bending each time she did this, then feel them spring back when she leaned forward once again.

In this relative calm I considered my possibilities. Accidents are always a shock, there is that first moment where your mind says "Uh Oh," but can't quite believe it, and so almost relaxes, then the next moment when the pain hits and the mind clenches tight around the idea that "Oh Shit, this is the end." Then what happened has happened, and your mind catches up with it and reassesses, saying, "I survived. I'm hurt, but it's not too bad." Then the next thing happens, because it is never quite over, and your mind realizes, "Damn, I may not be clear of this yet." I was at that point, with the horse standing on me, where I had to consider that even though I was still alive and not too bad off, things could go from bad to much worse in a matter of seconds and it could depend on me.

I gingerly grasped the fetlock of the foot which stood on me, hoping the mare didn't panic at my touch and begin to kick me to death. She gave a violent start and froze. I slowly began to twist my body sideways as I pushed her foot off of me. She never picked it up, I had to push it off, taking a lot of my skin with it. As soon as the foot went off me and struck the ground, the spell was broken and she exploded again, rearing back with such force that she finally broke the rope which held her and she tore away, kicking dirt and leaves in my face.

She charged around the corral in such a state of panic that she scared Gravy into snapping his rope and the two of them ran in circles, trying to get out, trying to get away from me, the human who lay where no human should be, on the ground in their corral. I had rolled into a ball, waiting for them to stop, but finally crawled to the snubbing-post in the center and wrapped myself around it for safety. I thought if I waited long enough, Mrs. Farley would come see if I was done yet and to give me my $30 check, $15 per horse to trim. She would find me injured and get help. Fifteen minutes later, I was still lying there with the horses chopping and dicing the dirt around me.

Lucky as I was not to be mincemeat, I knew I couldn't stay there forever. It was getting harder to breathe and I feared my lungs were filling with fluid. I used the post to pull myself to a standing position and tried to catch my breath. Once I was on my feet, the horses stopped running. Milling in a corner, snorting, wide-eyed and dripping sweat, they stared at me, heads held high. I don't blame them for staring. I was a mess, filthy with dirt, leaves, sticks and blood. My clothing was torn and I was bruised and scraped. Dizzy and nauseous, I began to walk towards the house.

Remembering my tools, I turned back and carefully bent and picked up each one, trying not to get knocked down by the scared and excited horses. I had paid $95 for the nippers, $15 for the rasp and $7 for the knife. I sure as hell wasn't gonna let Biscuit and Gravy churn them into butter while I was being taken to the hospital!

Standing at Mrs. Farley's front door about twenty excruciating minutes later, I rang the bell. She opened, the phone receiver on a long cord held against her ear. Dressed in snow white mini-skirt and flouncy tennis blouse, her makeup freshened and her bleached blond hair pony-tailed with a white scrunchie, she was the picture of a country club wife.

"There you are, dear, I was beginning to wonder what happened to you!"

"Your horse stomped all over me," I said in a gasping voice.

"Oh, my God!" Mrs. Farley said, looking at my feet. "Is your foot all right?"

"Not my foot," I wheezed, "my chest."

The quizzical expression on her face was almost humorous. "I have to call you back," she said into the receiver. Her roving eyes took in my ashen face, the twigs and leaves in my hair, the dirt on my shoulders. A little while later, we were in her BMW, driving entirely too fast down through the foothills to Kaweah-Delta Hospital. An hour drive and two hours of waiting in the Emergency Room, during which time I could only take shallow painful breaths and no one even looked at me to make sure I wasn't dying of a punctured lung, I finally got x-rayed.

Not only had three ribs broken but my chest had been compressed, tearing muscle and ligament all around my rib cage. Eventually in the days that followed, a deep bruising would appear between my scapulae, matching the one across my sternum. It would be two years before the aching and pulling in my left chest and side would go away.

The doc sent me home with some codeine which jangled my nerves and barely touched the agony, no wrap ("We want to encourage deep full breathing to facilitate healing") and instructions not to do <u>anything</u> until the pain went away. Not to do anything? That's right, not anything! Certainly no dirt-shoveling in a trench, laying pipe and running a big vibrating monster like a Rammax!

So much for doctor's orders!

Amy R Farrell

3

Shovel Jockey
In which I master the art of muck-sticking

Well, I had been busted by a rank horse and life had busted me from the rank of professional farrier to the rank of shovel jockey. At the time I thought it was a temporary condition but major life changes are very often initiated in seemingly innocent ways; getting busted by a horse, responding impulsively to a rumor of easy money to be made on the mountain job, saying, "Anything," to a question from a new boss.

I had thought I would flag traffic for a few months, pick up a few bucks until I could get under a horse again. I hadn't counted on the fear. The hind end of a horse terrified me, unless it was that of my own black Arabian mare Dreamer, in whose vocabulary the words spook, kick and explode did not exist. It would be years before the memory of Biscuit's flying hooves (as seen from underneath) would fade. As for flagging, I never did end up being a flagger on "the Sierra Project," although I did on other jobs. I ended up being such a good laborer, even with broken ribs, that I ended up doing it for the next ten years, through the Laborer's International Union of North America. In all that time, I only met one other woman construction worker.

I ran the Rammax, but in between compactions, I helped Placido and Juan, the other venerable old man on the job, "soap and slip" six-inch ductile iron pipe in 16 foot lengths lowered to us by a boom-truck operator. Placido was a sweet old guy with a round face, chipmunk cheeks and those pretty hazel eyes. His friend Juan was thin with elegant hands, a smooth chiseled face and deep laugh lines around his mouth.

They waved me to them when it was time to lay pipe and schooled me through the procedure. At lunch, they shared with me the soft tortillas that their wives made with their own hands and the salsa made with peppers they had grown in their gardens. When the other men on the job treated me badly, Placido would remind me, "*Esta bien, Eh-mee. They are only men, they are not saints.*"

After several lengths of pipe were laid, the front loader man would dump piles of fines (native soil which had been run through a sifter to pick out the roots and rock) over the pipe. I would jump in, push the tops off the piles with a few forward strokes of the shovel, throw my back against the trench wall, stab straight down into the pile and pull the dirt towards me with a motion like rowing a canoe. Going quickly down the trench, moving dirt in this manner and stomping and shoving dirt with my feet, I could get a lot done before the water truck roared by, spewing water to aid compaction.

The water truck guy thought it was a hoot to douse anyone he could. Hopefully, you had enough time to clamber out of the trench and get clear. And if you didn't lay your jacket and lunch-box far enough up the bank, the water truck guy would wet that too. Everything on the Sierra Project was bing bang boom. I did every part of the laborer's job, shoveling (or mucking, as it was called), slamming pipe and running the compactors. There were a couple of vibro-plates for compaction too, but no one but me touched the Rammax. Skip had put me on it, after all.

There were several other laborers on the job. In fact there were about ten at any given time and only about eight shovels. This was done on purpose, I came to believe, as a way of weeding out slackers. If you set down your "muck-stick" for a minute to do something else, then the fines were dumped and everyone grabbed for a shovel, you might be left empty-handed. If Skip, passing by, noticed you were not shoveling, you would be tramped off. Skip sent home about two a day for the first four weeks and each morning a few more would be sent up from the union hall. I saw this happen to several men and though I think Skip would have liked to tramp me, he never had cause. It was in this manner the final crew was assembled. Only the ones who were "Johnny on the spot" would stay.

The new laborers who arrived each morning were called FNGs by those who were already on the job. This was military slang and meant "Fucking New Guys." The implication was that since you were not likely to last very long, no one would recognize you as a crew member until you'd proven you had what it takes. I survived each culling, in part because I saw right away what was going on and held on to my muck-stick, even if it meant shoving it through the ring on top of the Rammax and putting up with the noisy vibration of it when the machine was running, or setting it on the ground near my hands when I went to help Placido slam the ductile iron. I also never slacked, no matter what. I worked as hard as I could all day long and kept repeating my mantra, "Come on, girl, don't get bucked off!"

At 5' 6" and weighing 125 lbs soaking wet, I had been active all my life and was in good shape. A backpacker who had logged a lot of miles in the high country, I had been in the Youth Conservation Corps during High School and had worked as a Seasonal Maintenance Worker for the National Park Service (NPS) after graduating. There had been a few years working as a stable groom for the U.S. Park Police in San Francisco which involved shoveling a lot of horse manure, and the previous summer as an Emergency Fire Fighter for the NPS in Sequoia National Park, plus the aforementioned horseshoeing school.

For an outdoorsy twenty-five year old female who had done physical labor before, the work was hard, but not too hard. I was shorter, lighter, and had far less muscle bulk than the men, but I made up for it with quickness and energy. I was doing the same work the men were doing, but I was doing it with three broken ribs and nobody knew that but me. Skip would've tramped me off the job if he knew I was impaired. The ribs were healed well enough when I started the mountain job that the bone ends did not grate against each other anymore but they ached constantly, a deep dark dull ache.

The pull of the shovel through the heaps of dirt tormented my injured body, but I needed this job! And if I lost it, my initial investment of $325 would be a waste. I could not afford to lose that money, especially since I still had to pay it back to the people I'd borrowed from.

I was a shovel jockey now, for good or ill.

4

Dutch And The Rammax
In which I tangle with an even ranker man

"**What's** that pussy doing on this job?" were the first words out of Dutch's mouth. It was about a week into the job when he arrived on the site, a burly ruddy-faced fellow with a reddish mustache and sandy hair. The way this guy swaggered in, you might have expected him to be wearing a shirt saying "The Greatest Laborer In the World."

Within minutes of arrival, he was bragging that he was a hard-rock miner by trade, had operated rock-drills on big hydroelectric jobs in the Sierras, like Wishon and Oroville Lake, working seven-fourteens (7 days a week, 14 hours a day) for months at a time without surcease, living in man-camps where men were men (and women didn't dare show their faces even to cook breakfast), drilling and blasting huge tunnels miles deep inside the mountain, operating the massive elevators that lowered full-sized heavy equipment and diesel trucks deep into the ground and working as a chuck-tender on air tracks and jack-legs, those noisy machines that drill holes in solid rock. He wore a round-brimmed brown fiberglass hard hat that was the hallmark of a miner and he was full of himself, that was plain from Day One.

I knew the moment I saw his cold blue eyes on me that I was in for it. "No pussy's ever been on any job of mine," he announced and he set about trying to get rid of me.

He tried to make sure I did not get a shovel.

I made sure I did.

He tried to out-muck me, moving more fines faster than I thought humanly possible.

I worked harder than <u>was</u> humanly possible and managed to keep up with him, my cracked ribs straining against the pressure.

He preached about the travesty of women on construction jobs, that me and my ilk (I was looking around for my ilk, but I didn't see any!) were only here to destroy the proud traditions of the trade unions, undermine a hundred years of hard-fought-for worker unity, spit in the face of those who had had their skulls cracked by the clubs of the company goons, emasculate every person whose genitals swung free in their trousers and cause the next Ice Age.

Well, maybe not that last one, but he might as well have added it! The men stood in a circle around him, catching the glib phrases that blossomed from his lips and sucking them down whole, cheering him on with a resounding chorus of "Fucking A!" and "Hell, yeah!," all the while glaring murderously at little ol' me.

During each of these recitations of my litany of sins, I just kept on working.

Dutch said a lot.

I said not one word. Just the little mantra running through my head, "Don't let 'em take your tools."

Dutch took one look at me running the Rammax and decided that the job was rightfully his. At every opportunity, he tried to beat me to the machine. He made sure that he worked the trench as close to the Rammax as he could to see if he could beat me to it. He stood stolidly in the trench and took the full blast of the water truck if it meant getting to the Rammax before me. Once I saw Dutch's tactics, I played by his rules. I got drenched a few times but I stayed with the machine. After the first time he did get to the machine before me, I vowed it would be the last. Skip had put me on it, after all! I'd be damned if some FNG was going to put me off it!

As far as that went, Dutch was the only man who came up on the job whom nobody treated as an FNG. It was obvious that his reputation around Local 294 was such that everyone was deferential to him but whether because he was a bully and a blow-hard or because they respected him as an experienced Laborer, I could not tell. One thing was clear, he was a hell of a strong man, with great physical endurance and a forceful personality and that miner's hat on his head spoke in big bold letters. In the parlance of the construction world, his balls were big ones and solid brass. That clanking you heard when he walked, that was them knocking together.

My friends Placido and Juan toned down their cordiality towards me. They had patiently shown me every phase of the job and guided me gently through some of the pitfalls. I still sometimes went to the head of the trench and helped them slip the ductile iron, but they no longer waved me over to them, big smiles on their brown faces. Perhaps it was only because they saw the ongoing battle over the Rammax and did not want to distract me, not because they had bought in to Dutch's view of me as the source of all evil on earth.

One day, the water truck whooshed by wetting both me and Dutch to the skin as the rest of the crew ran like rabbits to get out of its way. Dutch shook off the water streaming off his wide-brimmed hard hat and set off for the Rammax. He was ahead of me in the two-foot-wide trench and I knew I could only get by him by aggressively pushing him aside. I took off at a run, but just before I bumped into his broad back, I threw my hands to the trench lip and vaulted my body up out of the trench.

Sliding like a baseball player, I skidded over the dirt and pushed myself feet first back into the trench ahead of Dutch. Landing in a cloud of dust and knocking dirt and debris into the trench with me, I raced to the Rammax. My hands touched the controls an instant before his. I grabbed hold of the levers tightly and turned to look up into his seamed and dirt-smudged face.

Mostly, I was looking to see if he was going to hit or grab me, thinking I might turn to see big gnarled angry hands reaching for me, tightening on my neck, dragging me bodily from the Rammax and throwing me to the dirt, but I found myself looking up into sea-ice eyes. His face was still, chipped from rock. The little lines around his eyes and mouth were fine white ones against the bronze of his laborer's tan and as he stared at me for a moment, I saw subtle changes occur. The fine white lines disappeared as the seams deepened and his face became a uniform brown. The eyes slitted up, almost closing, and the stern straight lips parted, slowly, as if reluctantly, showing a crocodile grin. His big broad shoulders hunched, the huge muscles bunching under the frayed dirty T-shirt. There was no sound, but all the signs were there.

Dutch was laughing!

"For a tiny little split-tail, yer a hell of a man!" he said.

A compliment, presumably. I cracked a smile. With caution.

His big right paw landed with a thud on my shoulder, and he shook me roughly, then bent and began picking up the rocks and roots I had knocked into the trench in my mad vault. Chucking them out, and tisk-tisking like a harried den-mother, he turned and walked back down the trench. I let out the breath I was holding and started up the Rammax.

On the third week an FNG sent up from the hall, a tall skinny forty-something who dropped his muck-stick, put his foot on it and lit up a cigarette every time Skip was out of sight, muttered a derogatory comment about me. I was in the process of shrugging it off, when I was startled to hear Dutch's voice, loud and clear, "She's twice the man you are, ya lazy mother-fucker! Say another word about her and I'll shut yer mouth for ya, sure as shit!"

"God damn," the FNG said petulantly, "I didn't know she was yer wife!"

"She's not my wife, Mother-fucker, she's a laborer! And a damn good one! Makes the rest of you sorry sacks of shit look like schoolgirls! If anyone deserves to be in my union, it's her! She can work circles around you lazy fuckheads. I don't want to hear another word!"

He didn't, either. The skinny FNG only lasted another day, because Skip spotted him standing on his shovel smoking a cigarette and most of the other sorry sacks of shit Dutch had referred to were tramped off within a week. By the fourth week, the culling was complete, the crew of the Sierra Project was assembled and we worked seven months together until the snow flew.

Dutch and I worked elbow to elbow all summer long, and became friends through the shared sweat of our brows and the mutual respect of two people who are good at what they do. Where Juan and Placido had quietly schooled me on quality of work, it was Dutch who had set the standard for quantity that I learned to live by. Keeping up with the man as he flew through every job of work built in me a stamina which served me well in my construction career.

Many men are big and strong, able to lift and haul great loads, but much of construction work is an endurance game. The big and strong often burn out fast where the lean and light go-go-go all day. I was lean and light and after a few months of mucking trench, I was pretty ripped as well. I matched Dutch stroke for stroke and honed my body like a blade. By the time the summer was done, I was a bona fide laborer!

Dutch had a wealth of knowledge and was a garrulous sort. We shared rides to the job as we both lived in Three Rivers, driving in his scrappy old 1972 Cadillac rag-top or my Toyota truck, so I learned all about the union, the various trades, about how to rustle up jobs, and about drilling and blasting.

When the Sierra Project ended, I stayed in the union reporting to whichever jobs the rep sent me out on when my name came up on the board. The board was quite literally a board with numbers on it, hanging on the wall at the hall, with name tags on wooden pins which would be moved closer to Number One each time a laborer or laborers got sent out. There were a couple hundred names on the board at any given time and it often took several months before your name would get to Number One.

The only way to circumvent this slow march towards eventual employment was to be name requested by a company for a given job. To do this, one had to "rustle" the job, which meant appearing in person at a project and convincing the foreman or superintendent to hire you, at which point said boss would call the hall and ask for you by name. It was through this method that I got most of my jobs but it was because of my work that I kept them. I just did the work, bottom line.

This was not the liberal-minded coed environment of the National Park Service in whose benevolent auspices I had worked since coming of age. In the profit-driven private sector there were no federal mandates to recruit and employ women in nontraditional jobs nor the tolerant attitudes of coworkers who were regularly reminded of the legal aspects of nondiscrimination. I was not indulged as a golden child of the new age.

In the highly competitive real world, all that mattered was completing the contract as quickly and cheaply as possible, passing the inspections and getting paid. Bosses cared for nothing else. We workers were cannon fodder. We either made money for them or we didn't. If I made it as a laborer, it would be because I was tough and could do the work.

I had to be at least as tough as the men around me.

Not really knowing what I was in for, I had grasped a thread and followed it into the labyrinth. Ahead, somewhere in the dark, lay the Minotaur.

I had stepped off into No Woman's Land.

5

The Hero's Path
In which I am rode hard and put up wet

"It's gotta get broke loose, that's the only way! We gotta be able to divert the water from the project!" the big shaved-headed black man, Pappy, told the foreman.

Dan, the foreman, took off his grubby white hard-hat and ran his fingers through his sweaty hair. "All right, all right, I didn't wanna have to do it but we're gonna have to! Damn, I was hopin' there'd be another way!"

"It's gonna be a bitch," Pappy said, "but somebody's gonna have to go down in that pipe. It's gonna be tight in there."

"Yeah, yeah," Dan agreed, "the kid'll have to go."

I looked up from my work, glanced at the two men, then at the only other person who, besides me, in this fraternity of grizzled over-forties, might qualify as "the kid," a lanky pimply-faced 18-year-old boy who stood about six foot one. He was looking up too, nervously drawing himself to his full height. He seemed to loom over me.

"Hey, kid, come over here," the foreman said, looking in our general direction. We both stood still, staring.

"Which kid?" I finally asked.

Dan laughed. "You, girl, come over here, I gotta little job for ya." I followed him, wondering what the hell I was in for. "You ain't claustrophobic, are ya?" Dan inquired as we walked.

"Uh, no sir, not that I know of, anyway."

"Scared of the dark?"

"No."

"Well, you have any trouble down there, you just give a little jerk on the line and Pappy'll pull you back out."

This was not sounding good. "Yeah, okay," I said, trying to sound casual. "That sounds like a plan."

Before I knew it they had strapped a heavy-duty leather and canvas safety belt around my waist, clipped on a long lanyard, and put a battery-powered headlamp on my hard-hat. Safety goggles, ear plugs and a bandana over my mouth and nose completed my safety gear. They clipped my lanyard through a ring welded on the backhoe bucket, swung the backhoe out over a huge crater dug in the ground and lowered me down into the crater, thence through a two foot diameter hole they had busted in the top of an underground storm drain. I dropped inside, my feet landing in about six inches of mud and wet leaf litter, my headlamp flashing off the interior of a four-foot diameter concrete pipe, complete with spider webs like a Halloween haunted house.

"Any water in there?" Dan hollered from ten feet up above.

"Some," I hollered back.

"Ya see it?" Dan wanted to know. "It" was the rotten plywood which had years before served as a makeshift form for the cement which had been pumped into this pipe to block it.

"Yeah, it's right here."

They lowered an electric Sawzall down to me on a rope, with the extension cord wired at intervals to the rope leading up to a portable generator. "Go ahead and see if you can cut the wood away from the cement."

I was standing in water, hunched over in a four foot pipe, in near darkness, with tons of hot uncomfortable gear on, holding a very squirrely tool. "Is this thing grounded?" I inquired nervously.

"Sure, kid, what do ya take me for?" Dan hollered.

I said a quick prayer, not exactly thrilled about the possibility of my name being featured in an article on industrial accidents, positioned the saw blade against a portion of the rotten plywood and pulled the trigger. The saw bucked like a rodeo bronc and almost put my ass in the water, but I braced my feet and held onto it. The noise, even with ear plugs, was deafening. Black widow spiders, daddy longlegs, one large wolf spider and an assortment of other creepy arachnids boiled out from behind the plywood as I cut chunks out of it. I hoped I'd get bitten so I could go home sick. Retreat with honor?

Between the Sawzall and a crowbar they lowered down to me, I had the plywood cleared away in about an hour, not counting the time it took for Pappy to replace all the blades I broke. The saw and the bar went up and down came a 5 gallon bucket for me to put the pieces in. Pappy hauled everything to the top in several loads. As he pulled up the bucket each time, I had to retreat further into the pipe so that the dirt and rocks that Pappy knocked into the hole would not hit me. I was having grim thoughts of being buried alive and hoped they had the excavation sloped enough so that there would not be a land slide. Up above, heavy equipment rumbled by almost constantly, sending showers of dirt and debris down the crater and into my little hole. This subterranean shit was certainly nerve-wracking!

"Can you see the concrete pretty good, now?" I heard Dan holler.

"Yeah," I said, running the beam from my headlamp over the surface. "How much did they pump in here?"

"No idea!" Dan hollered back, "it was so many years ago, no one is still around who knows! We're gonna send you a jackhammer and see if you can break through it! Move back from the hole!"

I pushed back into the dark shadows, feeling spiderwebs breaking all along my back and neck, and waited for the jackhammer to be lowered on a thin yellow nylon rope. It clicked, then thudded to the floor. I scrambled forward and untied it, then stood back while they fed the air hose down to me. Hooking the air-fittings together, I carefully wired the couplers together to prevent the air pressure from separating the air line from the hammer. If that happened, I could be clubbed to death by a whipping air line in a confined space. The jackhammer proved to be a 65-pounder. Hard enough to use vertically in a standing position but a real trick to use horizontally in a crouch. Luckily, despite the plywood form, the surface of the concrete was bumpy and lumpy in places. I would find a foothold for one foot, use every ounce of strength I had to maneuver the jackhammer up onto my leg, and trigger the mechanism. The jackhammer would blast about three or four strokes before it and my leg would fall off the wall and I would repeat the procedure.

"How ya doing, kid?" I heard Dan holler down at me after about the first hour of this backbreaking procedure.

"Just great!" I lied, crouching in mud, panting dust, sweating bullets and gripping the handles of the heavy machine which lay in the rubble at my feet.

"If you need anything, just let Pappy know. He'll be right up here. Oh, and kid, there may be water on the other side. We don't know how much, so when you break through, if you get any water, have Pappy pull you out so we can see what happens."

I gulped hard. "Yeah, sure, Dan, I'll do that."

I worried about that for the next few hours but then it became clear the threat was not imminent. The concrete plug turned out to be about three feet thick, sloping down to various thicknesses on the far side where there was no form. I crouched inside that pipe for a week blasting away chunks and filling a 5 gallon bucket with debris to be pulled out by Pappy and dumped. Sometimes large pieces would break free and sometimes the concrete would simply disintegrate into powder. There were a lot of voids and rock pockets in the concrete since it clearly had not been vibrated in, just pumped loosely. I asked Pappy for a 10 pound sledge hammer with about a foot cut off the handle. This I used whenever the jackhammer was impossible, like for the fringe of concrete coming down from the ceiling. They got me a small military biffy shovel to scoop up the powdery debris. I wore so many holes in the fingers of my gloves, I took to duct-taping them.

At the end of each day, I would emerge, some Gollum-like creature from the depths, my goggles removed revealing clean circles around my eyes in an otherwise filthy gray face. I could barely stand upright for the aching of my back and quads and my ears would ring all night. Showering when I got home, the water would run like chalk down the drain, and my cleaned skin would show multitudes of small black bruises from the heavy jackhammer where it had bounced and jounced along the length of my thighs and the sides of my calves.

"Beat to shit," I would mutter as I soaped up and rinsed several times to get all the filth off. "I oughtta quit this stinking job!" But each morning, the alarm would ring at 4 a.m. and I would suit up to go back to the job. Eighteen dollars an hour plus benefits paid into my union accounts was a powerful incentive, not to mention my own dogged determination to not be a quitter. I admit there were moments when I lamented having ignored the entreaties of my high school guidance counselor, Mr. Wallace, to apply for scholarships to go to college. Having high reading comprehension, a quick mind and an ididic memory, I was able to breeze through most of my classes with minimal effort, as long as I avoided my nemesis, math. English, history, literature, foreign language, composition, speech, drama, art, these were easy for me. I had been an "A" student but a lazy one. Well, I mused, as I pulled up my bootstraps for another day in the hole, I ain't lazy now! Can't afford to be.

I had grown up in Mill Valley, California, in the sixties and seventies, a bastion of liberal intellectualism, observing at my parents' table the rapid-fire political debates of sophisticated professionals: Architects; engineers; college professors; artists and writers. The people of the mind were familiar to me, those humans who made their way in the world through the fruits of thought not of labor.

They were the ones, who if they appeared on a construction site, were seen in spotlessly bright orange vests over white-collared shirts, wearing shiny unscuffed hard hats and carrying clipboards in the crooks of their arms. They tripped carefully over debris in polished shoes, observed the people of the body sweating and slaving in the dirt and the dust, made a few ticks on the clipboard and beat a hasty retreat to locate a restaurant which served a decent two-martini lunch.

Their work was in the realm of ideas and concepts, plausabilities and feasibilities. The people of the body? Their work is in the real-time world of rock and steel, dirt and concrete, wood and nail, flesh and bone.

The realm of realities.

The mind people were my people and I felt at home among them, yet when the critical moment came and I should have waltzed away to college with the rest of the children of the mind people, I stubbornly bolted in the other direction. I wanted to get on with life! I wanted to get into the thick of things! I wanted to get my hands dirty!

Well, they were sure nuf dirty now. Along with all the rest of me. But no complaining. I wasn't here 'cause anybody had fooled me.

For better or for worse, this was the life I had chosen, and one thing about me, I throw myself headlong into every experience! If it is worth doing, it is worth doing to the max. Boots laced up, hard hat on, once more into the breach...

Another day of blasting, smashing, filling, blasting, smashing, filling, blasting, smashing, filling, sweating inside a 4 ft pipe. Loud! Debris pinging off the interior! Chunks striking my face! Breathing concrete dust! Dark and spooky! Fear of being buried alive! Spiders! Backbreaking! Shoulders aching! Miserable!

This little job of work made regular construction work look like a picnic in the park. Why me? I wondered in my misery, watching the rest of the men walking off to their respective duties which left them above ground in the sunlight and fresh air. Oh, happy men! Oh, miserable me! Why me, oh merciful God?

Why? The answer was simple. It wasn't necessarily that I was a girl, although that was probably part of it. It was also that I was the smallest member of the work crew. This being smallest thing was going to land me in some tight spots.

For one thing, at least, I was grateful.

There wasn't any more water in that pipe.

6

Being Smallest
In which my diminutive stature predestines me for certain unsavory tasks

Girls aren't taught how to throw their bodies into things.

Boys grow up sliding into bases, putting everything they have into the throw of a ball. Girls? We're taught to be meek and to talk about our feelings. Showing up on a construction job, female <u>and</u> the smallest person on the crew, I found out quickly that, one, my feelings didn't matter, not a whit, and two, unless I did throw my body into things, I didn't stand of chance of making anything move. Everything on a job is built tough and heavy, tools are solid and well-made, cement sacks are big and heavy, lengths of boards and thicknesses of plywood are all designed to withstand great pressures. A little gal on a big job has a lot of heavy things she has to move and she can't move them unless she heaves herself into everything, throws what little weight she has against whatever she is trying to move.

This is hard to teach a person in whom society has instilled a message of gentleness and softness. Luckily, I had had horses. Horses are somewhat like men, big lunkheads that think they are in charge. No honestly, I really like horses. And they are nowhere near as lunkheaded as most men, especially most construction worker men. But leading a 1500-lb animal around on a 6-ft piece of rope as a skinny thirteen-year-old taught me how to throw my weight around and bucking 80-lb hay bales had given me a glimpse of what hard work the world was made of.

Building trails with the youth corps had shown me that moving rock and dirt involved more than just the hands and arms. Swinging a pick-maddock into chert rock required the whole body. Pushing the heavy contents of a full shovel brought into play the legs and back as well as the arms. I'd even learned at a fairly young age to use my right thigh to lift and push the shovel, a trick I would use to good effect during my construction career.

Being smallest landed me some strange assignments. There was the job where I was attached to a winch and lowered and raised up and down the steep sloped sides of the Friant Kern canal (emptied) so that I could sandblast the surface and then apply a sealer to cracks and fissures with a pneumatic caulking gun. My coworker manning the winch got to lean against the truck all day, spitting sunflower seed hulls and triggering the winch mechanism or loading bags of sand into the hopper of the blaster, or dropping cubes of sealant into the burner to be melted into hot caulk. Or he would get in the truck and drive another 20 feet along the canal. Meanwhile, I'm rappelling down the canal side in a full blast suit and respirator, dragging a stiff heavy hose and trying not to sandblast my own boots!

Being smaller than the men landed me one assignment on a job at Lemoore Naval Air Station in the great San Joaquin Valley of California, working flat on my back (not what you're thinking!). I worked day after day in an underground bunker with the weather in excess of 100 degrees outside (no telling how hot in the confined space of the bunker) scraping all the paint from the pipes and pumps of the jet-fuel pumping equipment. In coveralls, headlamp on, with protective goggles, shimmying around in tight spaces, I applied heavy-duty solvents (which dripped all over me) to the machinery, then scraped and wire-brushed the paint off, cleaned the work with TSP and a sponge, then finally brushing on fresh oil-based paint (without drips, mind you!). A tedious, uncomfortable and lonely job, breathing fuel, paint and solvent fumes and trying not to space out.

The boss came down the ladder into the darkness one day and didn't get an answer. He had to call me several times before I responded from the depths of my vapor-induced stupor. That was the day he rented a ventilator blower to force fresh air into the bunker. Bosses are cheap and will always save a dollar where they can. I suppose he realized he might end up with a brain-dead employee on his hands and really have some explaining to do. Whatever his motive, I appreciated the blower. Lots better after that.

There was the time I had to go check on a pump malfunction at a sewer plant. I climbed down a rung ladder 60 vertical feet underground with only a headlamp, Bing! Bing! Bing! down the ladder, the circle of light above getting smaller and smaller, the face of my coworker looking down to watch my progress getting harder and harder to recognize. Wearing clunky ill-fitting waist waders which slipped and slid on the metal rungs. The ladder descended a tube about four feet in diameter. Every 20 feet there was a mesh platform with a trap door allowing access to the next level, presumably to catch you if you fell. Why I was going down rather than my more experienced coworker, I did not know, as I didn't know how to repair the pump anyway. Reaching the bottom up to my waist in sewage overflow, I hollered the results of my investigation up to the man peering down, a conversation that went loosely like this: No, the pump isn't pumping.

Yes, there is a sewage leak.

Yes, but how do you feel?

I feel fine, damn it, but I stinks down here and it is disgusting standing in shit even if I do have waders on.

But you feel fine, otherwise?

Yes, I'm peachy and how are you?

Okay, I'm coming down.

Turns out I was being the "canary" for my coworker who waited topside to see if I would drop dead from methane gas. Not only small, but expendable.

After being in the Laborer's Union a couple years, the arcane language of 245s, transfers, belly-dumps and Rammaxes was now my language and I spoke it fluently. As well as jobs in the great central valley of California, I worked on several jobs in Sequoia and Kings Canyon National Parks and Sequoia National Forest. I was most happy working in the mountains. Living in Three Rivers, the little town right at the gateway to Sequoia, I considered any job in the Park to be in my backyard. My turf, as it were, and I would rustle hard to get on it.

It always caused quite a stir among the men when I showed up to rustle a job. Appearing in work clothes, with gloves, hard-hat, lunch box and a 25-foot tape measure on my belt at least half an hour before start time, I'd find the boss and ask him if he had work for me. The men would start in immediately. As far as they were all concerned, without even seeing me work, I was unqualified for the job due to being genitally-insufficient. To these guys, it was a package deal. If you didn't have the package, it didn't matter what you did have in your toolkit. The raw comments, propositions, cat calls, complaints and even threats rained down on me. As hard as it was to be the brunt of so much hostility, I stood straight and let it all roll off my back. I figured, given time and getting to know me, like Dutch all these guys would realize I wasn't so bad, that I was just another Laborer trying to make a living. Meanwhile, they could hate me all they wanted. I was here to work.

Sometimes a boss was willing to try me that very day, but if not, I would show up day after day, in some cases for a week or more, but invariably I would get put to work. Persistence paid off. Eventually someone on the crew would get culled, or call in sick, or get injured, or leave for some other reason. Eventually, the work load would increase for some foreseen or unforeseen reason and my services would be needed. I was already there, ready to work. All the boss needed to do is put in a call to Darce Daniels at the hall and ask for me by name.

Once hired, all I had to do was make the company money. Even small and female as I was, it wasn't that hard to make the company money. All I had to do was go-go-go all day, like a little Arabian endurance horse running the 100-mile Tevis Cup race, "To finish is to win!" and I left plenty of big strong men in my wake when I was on the business end of a muck-stick!

I can't even remember the details of all the times I was told to straddle the boom of a Gradal machine or step into the bucket of a massive excavator then be swung out over an abyss, to perform some little job of work, whether to pump-spray wax emulsion over a newly-poured concrete structure or to remove plastic plugs from steel-ply forms and slide greased she-bolts through or to dry-patch rock-pockets after forms were stripped from an overpass or a freeway bridge we had built. With little precaution taken to provide for my safety, I was tossed at jobs both difficult and treacherous, to universal cries of "Let the girl do it, she's small. Let the girl do it, she's light as a feather!"

I often mused, as I was being hoisted impecuniously over the streaming traffic of a freeway or dangled precariously over some parapet with a thirty-foot drop into the belly of an empty sewer plant below me, my tools clutched in my white-knuckled hand, how, for a bunch of fellows who are constantly reminding me that women don't belong on these jobs, can they persistently discover little jobs for which, of all the assembled crew, I am most suited?

Far be it from me, I decided, to argue with their experience and greater knowledge of the construction trades. If they thought I was the best person for job A or job B, I was not going to quibble. I would pick up my grip and climb on board, even if it meant be hung upside down by a lanyard with the foreman on his belly holding my feet while I stuffed expansion felt into a joint that had been neglected (by wiser heads than mine) during the forming process.

If they harbored any illusions that assigning me these unsavory tasks would cause me to cut and run, they were wrong. In fact, if such was their intent, they did me a kindness by offering me a chance, not only to gain the work experience (the credentials, as it were) of a seasoned laborer but also to prove them wrong in their belief that women cannot do what they do. I became the very person they were trying to prove I could not possibly be.

When I became a laborer, I made a pact with myself. Never turn down a job, no matter how shitty. If you don't want the shit jobs, don't be a laborer, join a different union.

If the men thought the work would be too hard for me, they were wrong. If I thought that the work would be the hardest thing about being a union laborer, I was wrong. The work was hard, but I was harder. I was a rock.

Maybe a small rock, but a rock. And I had to be able to handle whatever came down the trench.

7

Speaking Of Rocks
In which I have an Indiana Jones moment

Standing up in the trench, I brushed the dirt from my gloves. Hearing a loud Crack! from the slope above us, where Roger was working with the excavator, I glanced up in time to see a big round boulder break free and begin to roll. Our trench was directly in line with its trajectory and I had a mental image of it entering the trench and rolling down it like the boulder that chased Indiana Jones in Raiders of the Lost Ark. The reality was, however, that it would roll into the trench and crush us all.

"Look out!" I screamed.

It was on the Sierra Project, my first job as a Union Laborer. Placido and Juan and I were laying a feeder line to tie in the pipeline we had been laying with a large water tank that sat up on top of this mountain. We had dug and laid pipe and back-filled section by section until we got to the base of the mountain. Now came the tricky part. The big tank was about fifteen hundred feet up above us. The Cat 245 excavator that Roger was digging trench with could track its way up a slope that steep but digging and swinging the load around would be very precarious. We knew we would have to lay each section of heavy ductile iron pipe working uphill, since gravity would be working against us if we tried to lay it downhill. Each section slipped one inside the bell-end of the previous, so going uphill was the only way.

The boom-truck which had lowered each section to us could not climb the slope, so Roger would have to dig a length of ditch, then track to the bottom of the hill and sling a 16-foot pipe from a chain on his excavator bucket, then track back up the slope to lower the pipe to us. Very slow, very painstaking work, and also very dangerous for the five laborers in the trench.

Before the run up the hill could even begin, however, a path had to be cleared. The mountainside was a forest, covered with fir trees, black oaks and pines, as well as logs and boulders blocking the way to the water tank. While the trees were not very big, they still had to be removed for the big 245 to maneuver.

The boss, Skip, didn't want us to stop laying pipe long enough for Roger to clear the slope so we laborers were in the trench as Roger tracked the big machine up the slope above us and began knocking down trees, pushing logs out of the way and clearing all obstacles. The trench was five feet deep and sloped back on the sides due to the soft nature of the soil, two foot wide at the bottom but about four foot wide at the lip.

As Roger's machine squeaked its lumbering way up the hill, I kept glancing up nervously each time I heard a Crash! Smash! Thud! from the slope above.

The excavator was facing uphill, rocking back and forth on its track-layers as the tall articulated arm with the bucket on the end swiveled this way and that, crushing thirty-foot fir trees and shoving them off to the side. Roger would push an obstacle out of the way then raise and lower the bucket like a big fist, hammering the object into the soft dirt of the forest floor to keep it from sliding or tumbling down the hill. Bang! Bang! Bang!

This is what he was doing when the boulder began to roll.

When I screamed, "Look out!" everybody looked up. There were two other shovel jockeys in the trench with us and it was instant pandemonium as everybody tried to scramble out of the narrow space. The easiest way out was at the head of the trench but Placido and Juan were closest to it and the old men were the slowest-moving. One of the two shovel jockeys shoved me hard and I ended up on my knees on the floor, my mouth full of dirt, while the two guys stepped over me and started trying to climb over the Venerables.

I was spitting out dirt and trying to scramble to my feet. Looking up, I could see no one was really getting anywhere but dirt and rocks were tumbling down into the trench from their desperate efforts to escape.

For me, things were happening like a VHS tape being played in slow mode. The boulder was rolling past the 245 and Roger saw it as it passed his enclosed cab. His dark eyes locked on the thing like a fighter pilot's sights lock on a bogie. The big excavator spun around on its tracks so fast that gravity rocked the machine, almost toppling it. The "knuckles" of the bucket punched into the ground and pushed, righting the monster. It slammed back down on its tracks and stabilized. The boulder was still rolling, starting to gain speed as it passed. Then the arm extended out and the bucket uncurled, the steel claws reaching, reaching, reaching.

Clang! The boulder came to rest against the steel claws and the arm pressed down, pinning it to the earth. The rear of the machine rose up off of the ground as the big machine overbalanced. The boulder was stopped, but the Cat was unstable. Roger's eyes lifted and he stared at us. He could not gesture, needing both hands on the controls but it was clear what he was saying.

Quick! Get the hell out of the way!

The two laborers scrambled out, then Juan, who turned to help Placido and me. I was the last one out. We all ran for the edge of the trees, into a safe area. Roger waited until we were clear, then slowly began to curl the bucket and wiggle the boulder back. Pressing down on the boulder and slowly drawing it back towards himself, he was able to right the machine and keep the huge rock from rolling down the hill at the same time, preventing the destruction of tools and equipment which were still in the trench. He pushed the boulder behind some trees to brace it, then dug a hole for it, rolled it into the hole and hammered it down. Good as new!

"Unbelievable!" I breathed.

Juan nodded sagely. "Yes, he is very good on dis machine," the old man said.

"Eh-mee, we are alive," Placido said, patting my arm. "Now, since God has saved us, we make some changes how we do tings! And we don care what de boss say."

After that, even though it took even more time and no matter what Skip said, we vacated the trench any time the 245 was on the hill digging or moving obstacles. The only time we worked on the hill at the same time as the excavator was when Roger lowered pipe to us and we had him work from below, not from above.

I didn't mind the excitement and danger of construction work. It added a flavor to every day that I had come to crave. Life would never again be safe, and boring, and ordinary. My life had always been about stories, from the adventure tales I read as a child to the ones I made up in my head. Now I was living stories, living my own adventures. I wanted to keep on living them.

I didn't want to die on the job.

8

Spud Wrenches And Harleys
In which I receive a marriage proposal

Sparky looked from his work as I approached. He was leaning over the worn and broken teeth of the massive trencher machine, whose huge chainsaw-like blade was reclined along the pine-needle-covered ground under a set of big sugar pines.

"Hey girl," Sparky said, wiping his straggling black hair from his face with a greasy paw, leaving a darker black streak over his already black cheek.

"Hey Sparky," I said, "I'm supposed to help you."

"Yeah, I know, I asked for you." Sparky handed me an 18-inch spud-wrench and said, "Grab ahold of that nut right there and lay back on it with all your weight while I try to break this loose, eh?"

Sparky was an oiler, a diesel mechanic who is in charge of fueling, servicing and doing field repairs of trucks and heavy equipment on a job. Oilers drive around the project site in a one-ton or larger truck equipped with fuel tanks and pumps, a boom winch, generator, welder, and other tools. They tend to be a breed apart, usually loner-types, often strange in appearance. True to their job title, they tend to be covered in grease. I have known oilers whose skin, not just on their hands but on their face and arms as well (and who knows about the rest of them) are perpetually black as a chimney sweep.

More than one of the "black" oilers I have known have had long dirty uncombed hair and beards as well. They are often bikers. Such was the one I was sent to assist on this given day.

Sparky had unloaded two big cardboard barrels of new teeth by the time I was dropped off at the trencher by the foreman. The teeth, when engaged for digging, are mounted on a linked metal band which moves along and round the bar. When the bar is lowered into the earth, the teeth cut through the soil just as a chain saw cuts through wood and piles the dislodged dirt on either side of the trench. As it digs, the operator drives the machine along on its metal track-layers. Due to everyday wear and the striking of roots and rocks in the ground the teeth must be replaced as the job progresses.

Depending upon the size of the trencher, trenches of varying depths can be dug with one. This was a large trencher, digging a 5-foot deep 2-foot wide trench for us. The machine reportedly cost the company $1500 a day to rent and so it was important not to have a lot of down time due to broken teeth.

We were getting a lot more broken teeth because the company was using a flat-lander tool in a mountain setting. I had told the oiler Sparky the very first day of the job that the trencher the company was spending so much money on would be nothing but trouble in these granite mountains. Sparky had told the project superintendent Don what I had said and Don had come down on me like a ton of bricks.

He had pulled me aside and said, "What makes a slit think she knows more than the job super about the project's equipment needs, anyway?"

"I don't know more, sir," I said, turning red in the face, "but I know something about working in these mountains."

"That trencher is rated to cut through rocks," Don said, as his veins popped out in his forehead under the plastic suspension band of his white hard hat. "We spec-ed it that way. We're not stupid."

"No, sir, but this isn't just rocks, this is a mountain made of rock," I said, wondering if this was going to be my last hour on this job and starting to do mental calculations on how much of my pay I had been putting aside and how long I could live off of it until I was able to rustle another job. "The trencher won't be able to cut through solid granite when it comes across it. It'll dislodge loose rocks and it'll go through old rock, like DG, but once it hits serious young rock, it'll be a dead stop to your job. This is the Sierras. Every company I have worked for in these mountains has had to blast. In fact, every company I had ever heard of that worked in these mountains has had to blast." I was remembering the stories Dutch had constantly spouted of mountain jobs, both old and new.

Don spat out a wad of chew. It landed on my foot. "Old rock!" he shouted. "Young rock! Bullshit. We're not blasting. Blasting is too expensive and requires special permits. We spec-ed this job with no blasting."

I took a step back, kicking the black wad off my boot. "I'm sorry about that, sir. Someone should have advised you better, because you'll have to blast, and you'll probably lose money if you spec-ed the job without blasting."

"That's not going to happen," Don stated flatly.

"We'll see, sir," I said, "but when you get ready to blast, talk to me because I have the name of a reputable blasting company that's local."

For some reason he didn't fire me on the spot. Maybe he wanted me around so he could gloat when he proved me wrong. I was thinking about that conversation as I walked over to the wounded trencher to help Sparky change the teeth.

I took the spud-wrench the oiler handed me and fitted it to the nut. "Well, girl, you sure made a fool of ol' Don," Sparky said as he removed a broken tooth and reached into a cardboard drum for a new one.

"How so?" I asked, already knowing what he meant.

"I got my ass chewed out because of all the down time on this damned machine. So I said they needed to send this hunk of iron down the hill and get a blasting crew up here ASAP and Don hollered at me that I sounded just like that idiot girl. I said she ain't such an idiot if she knew more about trenching in the Sierra than whoever spec-ed this fucking job."

"Oooh," I said. "So, which one is gonna be going down the hill, me or this damned machine?"

"Don't worry," Sparky said, "you're a money-maker, unlike 'this damned machine.' They're stubborn fools but they're not idiots. Once it starts hitting 'em in the pocket book, they wise up. They want us to refit the trencher and get it ready to be shipped down the hill tomorrow, good as new. On Monday they're gonna start blasting."

"Really?" I said, fixing my spud-wrench onto the next nut. "I told Don I knew the best local company, Three Diamond, but he never asked me. Maybe I should go tell him."

"Girl, don't even bother. They may have decided to blast, but they don't want to admit that you were right. They've already lined up someone."

"Hmm, I hope they're good. Especially here in the Park. The Park officials are pretty particular about how things are done."

"Yeah, well, don't worry your pretty little head about it."

"I'll try not to," I said, with a laugh. "I guess I'm just a worry wart. There are a lot of park visitors here. Blasting is dangerous."

"No shit."

We worked a while in silence, then Sparky looked up at me in a serious way. "Amy, I wanted to ask you. Would you ever consider going with a man?"

I stopped working and stared at him. The grease-blackened face was looking at me, blue eyes bright in the dark face. "What, like you?"

"Well, yeah, me," Sparky said, "you don't think I'd ask for some other Joe, do you?"

I sputtered a little. "Well, Sparky, you know...I'm..."

"Oh, that. I just figured that was temporary," he said.

I fixed the wrench on the next nut, wondering to myself how it was that these men always think they know what is best for me or what, for me, is temporary. "No, it's not temporary," I said, "it's kinda like just the way I am."

"But you like motorcycles," Sparky said.

I had recently taken to riding a 1981 Kawasaki 250 up and down the mountain from my home to work as a way of saving gas, and had laughed with Sparky on more than one occasion when I parked my tiny little rice-burner next to his huge hulking Harley-Davidson.

It was certainly true that I liked motorcycles, which, arguably could have been further proof that I was in fact, not straight, therefore I was unclear what liking motorcycles might, in Sparky's mind, have to do with whether or not I would ever "go" with a man. I was dying to find out, if only out of pure intellectual curiosity.

"I love motorcycles," I said. "What does that have to do with it?"

"Well," he said, brightening, "the way I see it, if you were with me, you wouldn't have to ride that little Jap bike anymore, you could ride on my Hog."

Ahhh. Now I see. "On the back of your Hog, you mean."

He pulled loose another broken trencher tooth and reached into the drum for a new one. "Well, yeah. Is there a problem with that?"

"I like to ride my own motorcycle, not ride on the back," I said, conversationally.

He tightened the new tooth and pointed his grubby finger at the next to be done. I fitted my wrench on the nut. "Well, I tell you what, Amy," he said. "You marry me and I will buy you your own Harley."

"Marry you?" I was amazed at how swiftly my being dropped off to help a coworker with a job of work had ended in a proposal of marriage.

He looked at me and I could see for the first time in his chimney-sweep's face the look of a man who was smitten. "Yeah, marry me. You want me to get down on one knee? I'm serious. Marry me and

I'll buy you whatever Davidson motorcycle you want. I think we're a pair. Think about it, we're both in the union construction trades, we're both hard workers, we're both tough as god-damned nails, we're both into motorcycles. Think about it. With both of us working these prevailing wage jobs and traveling around the state, we could make a shit-ton of money! Take trips on our bikes in the off-season. We could work our asses off and retire young! I'd marry you in a minute! You're smart and you're pretty."

This long-winded liturgy of our common virtues and my personal attributes was unexpected from a normally taciturn man. I blushed deeply and fumbled with my spud-wrench.

"Well, what do you say?" Sparky looked at me imploringly, the whites of his eyes stark against his grease-black face. The image of him and me on our wedding day flashed in my mind. Sparky in a black suit covered in grease with his tangled matted hair and beard, somber visage black as a coal miner at the end of a 14-hour shift. Me in white gown and veil. His grubby hands with the black fingernails pushing a ring onto my white hand. You may kiss the bride. Yikes! And what about the wedding night? Was his you-know-what as sooty and greasy as the rest of him? I already had no desire to interact with a perfectly normal and clean you-know-what... much less...Oooh-doggies.

"Sparky," I said, with as much sincerity as I could fake, "that's a very attractive offer, but I have to decline. I am not really into men and besides I am with someone now, I mean, like living together and all."

"You think about it."

I shook my head. "I already know."

"You just think about, okay? Tell me you'll think about it."

He looked so sad, I told him I would think about it.

Poor Sparky! I hadn't meant to shake up his world when I showed up on the job. I was only trying to make a living, same as him. I was only trying to be myself. I certainly never meant to be a heartbreaker!

To this day I wish there had been another way to get that Harley.

9

Shot-rock and Sequoias
In which a hard rain is gonna fall!

"**We're** gonna start blasting today," Don said to me on Monday morning. "The flaggers are gonna hold traffic on the road while we blast that section of rock we hit just adjacent to the General Sherman Tree driveway. I need you to go to the Sherman Tree parking area and stop any hikers or visitors from coming down into the blast zone from those trails up there."

I was familiar with the trails he was talking about, having hiked and snow-shoed there many times. One led up from the parking lot to the General Sherman Tree, a giant Sequoia that was not only the largest tree on the planet but the largest living thing on the planet. The Sherman was a must-see stop on any park visitor's itinerary. The other trail was the Congress trail, which crossed the creek and made a loop through groves of Sequoia trees named after congressmen, presidents and generals.

There were actually three trail heads I would need to watch and the distance between each was several hundred feet. "I think I need another person," I said.

"You can handle it, slit," Don snapped, "or do I need to get a man to do the job?"

"Okay," I said, not willing to argue. "When is the blasting going to begin?"

"Just as soon as they can load the charges," Don said, referring to the fly-by-night company they had hired, rather than the one which I would have recommended if he had asked me.

"So, I'll wait for the three minute warning and stop anyone from coming down? I might need to know sooner than that, maybe ten minutes."

Don snorted. "Three minutes'll be enough."

"They have an air horn?"

"No," Don said, "they'll blow the truck horn."

I almost laughed, thinking he was joking. He was serious though. "I may not hear a truck horn," I said. "I'll be way back by the trailheads."

"That's not my problem if you go wandering off into the woods," he said.

I realized the man had not even driven up the Sherman Tree driveway to look at the area. He had no idea of the task he was asking me to do.

"All right," I said. "I'll handle it."

"Just don't let anybody down into that blast zone, or it'll be your ass," he concluded.

It was still pretty early in the morning when I first got there. There was no one around yet and I walked back and forth between the three trails. The Sequoia grove was quiet and peaceful aside from the far-off sound of the blaster's rock drill. Fir and pines were interspersed between the massive rusty-red trunks of the Sequoias and I heard the singing of birds as I walked on the soft springy needle-carpeted forest floor. A peleated woodpecker swooped down in front of me, then landed on a nearby tree. It cocked its crested head at me.

"Good morning!" I called cheerfully to the bird.   Breathing deeply of the cool sweet conifer-scented air, I thought, this is the life for me! Getting paid good money to hang out in the woods!

The General Sherman Tree was resplendent in the morning light, its cinnamon-colored bark vivid against the deep green of the surrounding forest.   At 36-feet in diameter at its base and 275 lofty feet tall, it seemed almost unreal.   No matter how many times I had gazed at these Big Trees over the years, I never quite got over them! Their trunks were so thick compared to their other cone-bearing neighbors that they could be something from the pages of a fantasy, like Tolkien's walking tree-people.   I stood about three hundred feet away from the Sherman tree and still had to tip my head all the way back to view its lightning-scarred crown.

Magnificent, ancient and beautiful all at once, it made me feel the presence of a masterful Creator.   I uttered a small prayer of thanks for being allowed the blessing of being alive in the presence of such awesome beauty!   If I turned my back on the driveway, the rest-rooms and the parking lot, and shut out the sound of drilling and the occasional whir of a passing car on the General's Highway, I could imagine myself a native person, perhaps a Yokuts or a Wukchumna, hundreds of years ago walking through this same forest, under these venerable trees, at one with the universe.   These very same giants had been standing, looking essentially no different than they do now.   I pictured myself, a deerskin-clad Yokuts, an acorn basket on my back. Or better yet, a bow in my hands, soft moccasins treading silently on the forest floor!

Looking down at my scuffed vibram-soled work boots and my worn blue jeans, the dream faded.   Here I was, a modern-day construction worker with a job to do! I straightened my plastic hard hat on my head and tightened the rigging with a crank on the little knob at the back. The brow band squeezed my forehead.   I jogged off across the parking lot to see what the blasting crew was doing.   This parking lot was removed in the years just preceding this writing and the area naturalized, with a new Sherman Tree access point created, but back then I could stand on the parking lot and peer down the high bank on to the General's Highway and see the trench we had dug to lay the pipeline, where the trencher had hit the hard young granite and been unable to continue.

A scruffy-looking man and a teenager, probably his son, were laying charges in holes drilled into the rock and running wires to a central blast box. The flaggers, out of sight around bends in the road, were letting traffic through one way at a time and cars were streaming by the open boxes of explosives, curious visitors craning their heads out of rolled-down windows to look at the proceedings. I shook my head, amazed at the carelessness of the company I was working for.

I watched for a while and then ran back over to the trails to look for people. When I did meet a hiker, I would inform them that we would be blasting soon and advise them to cut their visit to the Sherman Tree short and vacate the area ASAP, then I would make sure they did. As the morning warmed up, more and more people were showing up and so I jogged back to the road and hollered down to the blast crew.

"How long you think?"

The grizzled man looked up. "Half an hour maybe?"

"Okay, good. I'm going to start holding people back pretty soon then. You're going to give a three-minute, then a one-minute, then a thirty-second, then an all-clear, right?" This was standard blast warning procedure and I shouldn't have even had to go over it with the man, but my impressions of the situation so far left a lot to be desired.

He shook his head. "Naw, we're just gonna blow the horn, count to thirty and shoot it off." I was stunned. This meant I had better start holding people back right way, since I would have virtually no warning and no time to gather them into a safe place before it went off.

"How far back do I need to be?" I asked, thinking that I had better know the answer to that question since so much else about this situation was iffy.

"Five hundred feet'll do." I doubled that figure in my mind. I wasn't going to trust this guy. Ed and Jody Farrell didn't raise no fools. I paced out a thousand feet from the edge of the bank and selected a large Sequoia tree to be my safe area. The tree's trunk was about 25 feet in diameter and I felt that the shelter its great bulk provided would more than insure the safety of myself and the visitors. And the visitors were coming fast now.

Hikers were appearing from the trails where they had hiked over from junctions of trails at Giant Forest Village and Crescent Meadow. I ran to and fro gathering up the visitors and bringing them to the big tree, placing them in the lee of its wide trunk and explaining that as soon as the blast went off and the all-clear sounded (would they remember to sound the all-clear?) they would be free to go. Most of the people seemed to enjoy the excitement of being corralled up in a safe area near a blasting zone, a story to tell their friends about their trip to Sequoia, but some of them were impatient and kept asking me what the holdup was.

Fifty minutes had gone by since I spoke to the blaster and I was gathering more and more people, with more arriving all the time. I was running up and down, dragging groups of two or three over and depositing them in the safe area. More than once when I returned, I would notice that a couple of the original ones had left. The novelty had worn off and they had shared their chewing gum and trail mix with each other and compared stories of their hikes and sightseeing, now they were ready to go!

Amidst the questions and complaints, I finally said, "Okay, if you all promise to stay here where it's safe, I'll go over and ask the blasters when it will be."

I left the safety of my thousand foot buffer and jogged to the bank. Looking down, I saw the man and his son in much the same position as I last had seen them, bent over their work. The super, Don, was standing there too, arms folded over his chest. The traffic was now stopped completely, a sign that we were getting close. From my vantage point, I could see what Don could not, a group of six visitors hiking up the road from the Village, evidently having gotten by the flagger without being seen. They crossed the road behind Don's turned back, mere feet away from the loaded charges, and were coming up the bank, taking a shortcut to the Sherman Tree.

"Hey!" I called, and frantically waved them to me. I had to corral them with the others at the safe tree. They came towards me and before I could explain to them what was going on, Don turned and glared at me. "Godammit, you idiot, don't bring those people over here! What the hell do you think you're doing?"

"I just need to know how long it's going to be," I said, deciding not to try to explain where I got the people who were with me. "It's getting hard to hold people."

"I don't give a shit!" Don screamed. "Now get those people outta here!"

I turned and quickly led the group back to the tree, explaining about the blast and that they would have to wait until the all-clear before continuing to the Sherman Tree.

It was another twenty minutes before the blast and I had resorted to yelling at the visitors three times in order to control them. I had about eighteen people by then and keeping them bunched behind the tree trunk was difficult. I barely heard the truck horn when they blew it. "Now!" I hollered, throwing my back against the tree.

A series of explosions rocked the still mountain air and squawking ravens burst from nearby trees, their wings clapping as they fled. "Whoa!" I heard several of my captives cry and saw them step from behind the tree to peer in the direction of the blast. "Get back!" I yelled but they ignored me.

Clack! Crack! Clack! The noises above my head momentarily diverted my attention from the people. I glanced up. Rocks the size of footballs were tumbling down through the branches of the Sequoia, bouncing from limbs and breaking stobs loose from a hundred feet up. And not just the safe tree, the entire forest around us was being hailed with chunks of granite crashing down through the trees, shattering limbs and smashing into trunks like mortar rounds.

Clash, crack, thwack!

The rain of rock and wood was striking the ground all around us. I grabbed my hard hat in both hands and dropped into a squat, protecting my neck with my arms. Thunk! Thud! Thunk! The sounds from falling blast-rock and broken branches landing on the forest floor mixed with the cries of the terrified visitors. In about two minutes it was over and everything that was going to hit the ground had hit the ground. I was alive. I was uninjured. One piece of rock was embedded in the ground about three feet from my right foot. It was the size of my hard hat.

My heart pounding, I stood up and looked at the people. Some had run off into the forest as the debris crashed down around them, some had stayed. The ones who had run off had been not any safer, since the shot-rock had landed as far as fifteen hundred feet away from the blast. But thankfully, no one was hurt.

But they were royally pissed off. They unleashed their anger on me, threatening all manner of dire consequences of my negligence. No one waited for an all-clear, they stomped off in different directions, with the majority of them walking straight down the driveway and into the blast zone, voicing their lousy opinions of me all the way. Before I knew it, Don was driving his pickup truck up the driveway and into the parking lot. Jumping out, he threw his hard hat at me and began to yell.

I dodged the thrown helmet (a lot easier than dodging shot-rock!) and stood my ground, waiting for him to shoot his wad. "What the hell where you thinking, letting those people watch the blast? They could have been killed! My God, you little bimbo! They're all running to the ranger station to make a complaint! They could sue the shit outta us!" Blah, blah, blah!

I let him wear himself out, then I crooked my finger and walked off for the safe tree. He followed me, muttering curses and saying, "Do you want me to write you two checks? Because I'll damn well go back to the office and write you two checks!" This was a threat to fire me, the first check being last week's and the second being whatever time I had in this week.

I got to the big Sequoia and walked around behind it. I gestured to the disturbed soil and stamped-in footprints where a score of people had just spent an hour standing and sitting and pacing around impatiently.

"This is where we were, sir," I said. "I kept them here until the shot went off." I pointed at the chunks of rock and fallen branches all over the ground, and pointed to a big Douglas fir about 100 feet beyond the Sequoia where a piece of granite the size of a softball was up in a fork between two limbs. "Once the shot went off and the blast-rock started falling, it didn't really matter that some of them ran, the rock was falling all over." I gestured back into the forest, where Don could see as well as I could, pieces of gray granite lying about on the forest duff. To this day, if you walk among the trees in this area, you will see pieces of shot-rock amongst the trees. I turned to him. "You want to give me two checks now, go ahead."

"Fuck!" he spouted. He turned on his heel, stalked off to his truck and drove through the parking lot, rocks crunching under his tires.

The following Monday, a new job super arrived on the job from the Bay Area. The National Park officials had insisted that Don be replaced and that a new blasting company be hired for the duration of the project, one that they approved.

The blasting company, when it showed up Tuesday to complete the botched job at the Sherman Tree entrance, was so good that never once during blasting operations did a single piece of shot-rock fall through the air. They worked on that project all summer because we were digging trench with a Cat 235 excavator after the trencher had proved worthless, and we hit a lot of solid granite. And gee, guess what?

The approved company was none other than Three Diamond, the very same company I would have recommended if Don had asked me! This was the kind of irony my Pop would've loved!

There were days on jobs, working with all those men, that I missed my father so very much. I would have liked nothing better, after a hard day's work, than to be able to call him on the phone, hear his gravelly voice saying, "Hey, Kiddo! Whassup?" I would tell him all my war stories of life as a female construction worker; rolling boulders, flying shot-rock, battles over Rammaxes, jerky job supers, and greasy marriage proposals.

I can hear my dad laughing even now.

PART TWO:

THE ECSTATIC DANCER

Great is life.. and real and mystical..

wherever and whoever,

Great is death…. Sure as life holds all parts together, death

holds all parts together;

Sure as the stars return again after they merge in the light,

death is great as life.

--Walt Whitman, Leaves Of Grass, 1855

I have to run fast to keep out of my past.

--Ed Farrell, sometime in the 1970s

Amy R Farrell

10

Last Call
In which I talk to my father for the last time

"U.C. Medical Center. How may I direct your call?"

"Edward Farrell, please? I don't know what room, but he's there for heart surgery."

"Please hold." I lean back against the wall to which the phone is attached and glance out the dust-streaked window to the yard, where a cowboy-hatted Jim walks a flea-bitten gray mare to a hitching post.

Click. Click. Then, my father's voice, sounding distant on the crackly old land line. "Ed here."

"Pop, it's me," I say, holding the receiver too hard against my ear.

"Kiddo! Where are you?"

"At school. At the horseshoeing school. I just wanted to call you before your surgery tomorrow. This is the only phone I could use." The wall is hard against my back, my neck and shoulder muscles are sore from the swinging of a two-pound hammer. My palm has a new blister that smarts. Outside, Jim ties the mare, says something to Mr. Newmar, our teacher, then bends to pick up the mare's right front foot.

"Well, I'm glad you called. I'm just getting caught up on some Poly stuff."

"You're still working on that?" I ask.

My dad's main interest for the past year had been the effort to develop a multipurpose community center and affordable family housing project out of the long-abandoned Polytechnic High School in the Haight-Ashbury district of San Francisco where he had taken up residence after my parent's divorce. The city had wanted to sell the property to commercial developers but my father had headed up a community effort to save the site for a use which would better serve the people of the Haight.

"Feinstein wanted a revision on part of it," Pop says, "and I'm trying to get it done before tomorrow. I won't be much good for a few weeks afterwards, you know, and I want to meet the city's deadline." Diane Feinstein was then Mayor of San Francisco.

"How's it going?"

"I'll have it done," he says. His voice sounds rough. "I was three hours late getting to the hospital yesterday and ended up just bringing Site Plan Ten with me, so I can dress it up in between meetings with the docs and some last minute tests. Jerry's promised to come pick it up this evening and deliver it to City Hall for me." He sounds tired but his tone is one of satisfaction.

"That's terrific, Pop."

"What about you?"

"We have our midterm examine tomorrow," I say, "otherwise I would've come up today to see you."

"Don't miss any school on the old man's account. I'm in good hands."

"Maybe I can come up on the weekend, or maybe next weekend, after you've had a few days to recuperate."

"That sounds better. I won't be fit company for a week or two. I went through this all before. I know how it goes."

I'm watching the men outside with the gray mare. Jim has her foot between his knees and a pair of nippers in his hands. He spreads the sharp steel blades wide and places the edges against the muddy overgrown sole of the horse's foot and begins to cut. The mare jerks her head up and throws herself backwards against her rope. Jim's black cowboy hat flies off as he bolts out from under her. He slams into Mr. Newmar as he escapes from under the pitching horse and the two grasp each other's arms as they get themselves sorted out. Meanwhile the mare is rearing and shaking from side to side trying to break free. Jim and the teacher stand in the safety zone, watching her struggle. I see Mr. Newmar's lips move. I know he is trying to soothe the frightened animal. I know what he'll be saying, for I have been at the school six weeks already. "Quee-it, quee-it, quee-it now," his soft voice would be murmuring. Soon the mare stops pulling and stands braced, her four legs spraddled, her flanks heaving. Mr. Newmar steps to her side and strokes her neck under her thin mane.

"So, how do you feel about your midterm?" My father's voice says in my ear. I shift the receiver to my other ear and rub the one I had been pressing it against.

"Pretty good, Pop," I say. "The written part'll be easy, I think. The practical's harder."

My father says, "Flying colors, Kiddo. Flying colors for you and me both tomorrow."

"Yeah, Pop, you and me both," I say.

"How are you getting on with the other students? Are you making any friends?"

"They're all right. They're mostly cowboys. They're not used to the idea of women horseshoers."

Pop chuckles. "Well, if anybody can handle a bunch of cowboys, it'll be my daughter," he says. I laugh too, sharing an old joke. When I was little and loved to dress up as a cowboy, Pop used to called me Billy The Kid. He said I was born wrong gender and wrong century but he was glad I was here and was who I was so he could know me.

"I was impressed with the texts you're studying," he goes on. "Pretty sophisticated material for a trade school." One week ago, Christmas morning, I had sat with my dad at my mom's house in Mill Valley and shown him my school books, Lameness In Horses by Dr. O. R. Adams, Professor of Veterinary Medicine at Colorado State

University, and The Principles Of Horseshoeing II by Dr. Doug Butler, Professor of Animal Science at Northwest Missouri State University.

"What's on the practical?" It is clear Pop doesn't want to talk about his surgery or his fear of it or the fact the docs have given him only a fifty-fifty chance of surviving it.

I will oblige him. I don't know how to talk about those things either. "We have to shoe half a horse, that is, one front hoof and one rear hoof with shoes we make ourselves, working with another student. One makes a shoe at the forge while the other is trimming and nailing their shoe. Taking turns."

Outside, Jim has dusted off his hat and put it on. He is watching Mr. Newmar nipping the foot of the nervous mare. The teacher takes his time, letting the horse put her foot down whenever she starts to squirm and stroking her neck, his lips moving, "Quee-it now, quee-it," then gently picking her foot up again. Two other students have wandered over from their forges to watch their teacher work; Sally, the other female in the class, with her bushy honey-colored hair tied back and a brown cowboy hat on her head; and Roger, a tall beefy kid with plain broad face and a John Deere T-shirt and matching ball cap.

"You know what you're doing," my father says in my ear.

"A lot will depend on which horse I draw," I say, while outside the gray mare explodes again and throws herself backwards. Mr. Newmar jumps nimbly out of the way. "Some horses are easier to work on than others. We get them out of the surrounding area, people bring them in for students to practice on. We get all types. Some come off the Tule Indian Reservation. They're pretty wild."

"Well, you've been working with horses a long time, haven't you?" my father says. It is true. My sister Elly and I had bought our first horse for $50 when I was thirteen and she was sixteen, an unbroken buckskin mare who was barely over 13 hands high. We had no truck and trailer, so we walked the mare seven miles on dirt roads over the hills from Muir Beach to Mill Valley to a pasture on Kite Hill where we would board her for $10 a month not including the hay, using our baby-sitting money.

The next day the mare dropped a foal we hadn't been expecting and the foal tumbled down a hill into a church parking lot and was taken to the animal shelter where it spent the first day of its life without a mother's teat. We only knew the mare had been pregnant when we arrived in the late morning to visit our new horse and found the placenta in the dirt of the paddock. After hours of searching for the lost foal, someone suggested we call the animal shelter. Yes, they had picked up a newborn that morning. We went in a friend's station wagon and picked up the tiny mouse-gray colt, whom we named Moonshadow after the song by Cat Stevens. Sonja, the mother horse, rejected Moon at first and we had to milk the mare and feed the baby with a bottle. This meant that for a few weeks, we would have to sleep on a cot in the paddock and wake every two hours to feed the colt. It was a little scary sleeping on the hill, which was six or eight blocks away from our house. Elly and I would stay overnight together or our mom would stay with one of us. Eventually, the mare took to nursing her baby herself. This was my first experience as a horse-owner.

Eventually, once Moon was able to keep up with his mother, it was time to break the mare to ride. We had no money for tack, so we fashioned an old leather dog leash into a bridle of sorts. Elly would give me a leg up onto Sonja's bare back and lead us up to the top of the hill with a carrot held enticingly in front of the little mare's nose. At the top, Sonja would eat the carrot, Elly would release her and she would turn and run down the hill to her paddock, with me clinging to her mane, my skinny legs wrapped tightly around her middle. After getting dumped off a few times and having my knee banged into the corner fence post more than once, I learned to ride and the mare learned to accept a rider.

One day when Elly let go of the halter, rather than running back to the paddock, Sonja turned the other way and we rode into the hills with Elly walking along behind us. Within days I was taking long trail rides on Sonja and we were galloping along, leaping over logs and creekbeds. Soon after, Elly bought a Thoroughbred ex-race horse at a livestock auction for sixty bucks. She named the horse Andrew. He was a sixteen-hand bay and had navicular problems and was barely sound enough to ride. But he had spirit! Elly would charge around the hill on his bony back, a red bareback pad in place of a saddle, her bleached-blond hair flying in the wind. I would fly along after on the little buckskin, bare feet drumming on bare flanks to make Sonja run faster, an old brown Derby hat crammed onto my head. My dad loved to come up on the hill and take snapshots of his daughters galloping around on their horses, with little Moonshadow streaking alongside on his beanpole legs.

Our father was an architect and city planner, a protégé of Richard Neutra. Besides his work for his firm, he did pro bono work for community projects. In Los Angeles in the early sixties, he was a driving force behind the fight to save the Watts Towers from destruction and the development of a community art center at the site. He worked with the Chicano community in San Diego to build a Chicano Park. He helped preserve the magnificent wilderness of what is now the Mineral King district of Sequoia National Park by preparing community-change projections that were used to defeat the Disney Ski Park project.

After moving to the San Francisco Bay Area in 1963, he organized a two-county-wide public participation process that resulted in the preservation of acreage which later became part of the Golden Gate National Recreation Area. He battled the San Francisco Redevelopment Agency and won the space on Buchanan Street to create a city park that won national prizes.

Where he currently lived, in the famous Haight-Ashbury District of San Francisco, he was a board member of seven different community organizations, including the Drug and Alcohol Treatment Center and the Food Program. In short, my dad was a workaholic, but his hard work was never for the sake of raking in the big bucks, but rather for the improvement of the lives of people.

My parents had raised seven kids, four of "their own" and three adopted from county-run adoption agencies. They were among the few at that time who adopted interracially and were often cited by proponents of interracial adoption to demonstrate the potential successes. Mill Valley, California, in the sixties and seventies was a quaint town on the verge of wide open spaces, under the shadow of the looming Coastal Redwood trees at the base of beautiful Mount Tamalpais with coastline of cliffs and white-sand beaches nearby, a growing community of artists and scholars within an easy commute of San Francisco.

We Farrell kids grew up with little money but lots of love and we learned to make our own fun. Elly and I made our own fun with a dog leash, a fifty dollar pony and a lame sixty dollar ex-racehorse. We roamed the rolling hills and the dirt back roads of Marin County on the backs of our horses. We cared nothing for pedigrees, shows and prizes, only the wind in our hair and the feel of horse flesh under our hands, the warm sweet breath of a horse against our faces.

Elly eventually moved on from horses to men, marriage and world-traveling, but for me, the horse fever had caught. In high school, I became friends with Colleen whose black Arabian mare, Dreamer, would one day be mine (I would own Dreamer for thirty years until her death in February of 2006), and after high school, I would get a job with the U. S. Park Police as a stable groom and horse handler where I would work for almost four years. Now, here I was, at the oldest horseshoeing school in the country, halfway through a course of study in Farrier Science.

"Well, you've been working with horses for a long time now, haven't you?" my father says.

"Yeah, I guess I have," I agree, shifting the heavy receiver to the other ear. I remember showing up at his apartment in the Haight some afternoons coming straight from my job at the police stable. Sitting with him in his cluttered kitchen drinking tea and eating ginger snaps with the horse hair still on my clothes, talking about the horses, the cops, and the work mucking stalls and grooming horses. His tortoiseshell cat, Nancy Drew Girl Detective, would jump from his lap to mine and rub and purr and slobber all over me, loving the scent of the horses. It was like catnip to her.

"Kiddo, you'll do just fine tomorrow," my dad says.

Outside, Mr. Newmar hands the nippers to Jim and unties the flea-bitten gray. He walks the mare in a circle in the muddy yard and then beckons for Sally to come hold the horse for him. Sally takes the rope and rubs the mare's forehead with her knuckles. Mr. Newmar picks up a foot.

"Thanks, Pop," I say.

"Just take your time, and do what you know," he says. "You'll be great."

"Thanks."

"That's my girl," he says. "Look, Kiddo, Doc just showed up. He wants to talk to me."

"Okay, Pop, I'll let you go then," I say, feeling my throat begin to tighten. "I'll be thinking of you tomorrow."

"Don't worry, I'll be fine. Just focus on your test."

"I know you'll be fine, Poppo. And I will."

"These U.C. guys are the best in the biz," he assures me. I can picture him with his hospital bed adjusted to the upright position, Site Plan Ten spread across his lap, a pencil in his hand and one more tucked behind his ear, winking at the doctor, who stands there with a clipboard.

"I know," I say. "I love you, Pop. I'll call you in a day or so."

"Love you too," he says. "Dagnab, dog my cats and Rowrbazzle!" he adds, a private joke between us. Cuss words from the Pogo comic strip we both favor, kind of a jocular way of saying, "Give 'em Hell!" or "Break a leg!" as theater people say.

"Rowrbazzle to you too, Poppo," I say.

I blink the first tear from my eye.

11

The Remedy For Worry
In which I hammer away at fear

Hanging the receiver on the wall phone, I lean my head back against the flyspecked white-painted paneling. Now there are tears in both my eyes. What if, I wonder, that is the last time I talk to my dad? "Damn!" I say aloud. "Damn, damn, damn!"

Beyond the dust-streaked window, Mr. Newmar, who doesn't like cussing of any kind, for any reason, hands the nippers to Jim and gestures for him to take over trimming the gray mare. Sally holds the halter rope and the animal seems more relaxed. In the long shed where the forges are, students move about in the shadows, tonging steel into coal fires, bending over anvils. Gray smoke rises from chimney stacks over the forges. Muffled by the window and wall is the constant ringing of hammers striking iron. Ding! Ding! Ding-be-ding-bing!

Mr. Newmar walks across the yard, his blue tennis shoes squishing in the mud. He opens the door and comes into the classroom. The hinges squeak as he closes it behind him. He smiles at me as he rubs his feet vigorously on the mat.

"All right, Amy?" he asks.

"All right," I say, pushing away from the wall and passing a hand over my eyes.

"Did you get a chance to talk to your dad?"

"Yes, sir," I said, "thank you."

"How is he doing?"

"Fine."

"Surgery tomorrow?"

"Yes, sir," I say. "He's had open heart surgery before, about ten years ago and it worked really well. He was one of the very first people to have the bypass..."

"How old is your father?"

"Sixty-three."

"Oh, he's pretty young yet, Amy, he'll be fine."

I'm thinking, yeah, young except for a thirty-year battle with the bottle which had ruined his health and aged him to the point that most people took him for a decade older. At least! His hair and beard are snow white and he's a dead ringer for Santa Claus, as round and jolly as Santa but unlike that icon of Yuletide, Pop is no saint. All who knew him knew he had a classic Irish temper, could hold a grudge and be an irascible bastard! In many ways, he was a divided man. He was much improved, both physically and temperamentally, since he had beaten the bottle finally six years ago. Was it soon enough to help? I wondered.

"He was a heavy drinker for a long time," I blurt out.

The teacher looks up from his shoes.

"But he quit drinking," I add. "He's been sober for about six years now."

Mr. Newmar reaches out and squeezes my forearm. "I'll say a prayer for him," he says kindly. I smile and nod, imagining what would my father think of that, a man who gave up religion after a childhood as an altar boy, a man groomed for the priesthood like every other firstborn male in his Catholic family going back into the Irish mists, a man who saw organized religion as the opiate of the masses. "Thank you, Mr. Newmar," I say politely, "I'm sure my father would appreciate that." My father would get a kick outta that, is what I'm thinking. He'd think it was a hoot that Amy's Evangelical horseshoeing teacher is praying for him.

The teacher passes me to walk to his desk. "What're you working on?" he asks casually. I glance at him, shaking the picture of my dad in the hospital bed out of my mind. "Um, my sliding plate and my jar calks," I say.

"Need any help on those?" Mr. Newmar is rummaging in his top desk drawer. Then he shifts some papers across the top of the desk, looking for something.

"No, sir, I think I know what to do," I say.

He looks up and smiles again, his blue eyes twinkling. "Best remedy for worry, Amy," he says. "Work."

"Yes, sir," I say and move towards the door.

"I'm sure your dad will want you to do well on your midterm tomorrow."

"I'm sure," I say and open the door. I walk across the yard towards the shed, my new Pecos-style pull-on workboots (all the horseshoers are wearing 'em these days!) squeaking as I sidestep the worst of the mud puddles. Arriving at my forge under the lean-to shed, I reach down and flip on the fan switch. The electric motor whirs and the air begins to pass through the coals, pushing the bright-orange fire through the jumble of black chunks. To one side of the hooded forge in a pile of gray ash lays my unfinished sliding plate, a shoe I will probably never make outside of school, having no interest in ever seeking my living among those who push their horses into the flashy but absurd sport of Reining, making them spin in tight circles and sprint to the other side of an arena only to slam on the brakes and slide 10 or 15 feet to a stop, then to spin in tight circles again. I pick up my tongs from the anvil and slip my forefinger inside the handles. I spread the jaws and grasp the sliding plate, pick the shoe up and poke it into the hottest part of the fire.

I glance around me. Under the shed roof, other students work their iron. Ding! Ding! Ding-be-ding-bing! The forges line both sides of the long shed, their chimneys crooked and extending out beyond the edges of the roof, a long central aisle in between. Out in the yard, Sally holds the gray mare while Jim and Roger take turns trimming her feet.

It is January 6, 1986 and it is not raining today, but the yard is still muddy from the rain of days before. Most days that it is not raining there is a heavy pervasive "valley fog" that doesn't burn off until noon.

Cold and damp, most students are heavily clothed until working at the forge warms them enough to strip down to shirt sleeves. Big Roger, he of the John Deere T-shirt, is usually the first one to strip off his warm layers. I wear my heavy National Park Service hooded sweatshirt with the hand-warming front pouch. I have been living in a tiny trailer at the nearby KOA Kampground, a trailer rented from the horseshoeing school, going home on weekends to my girlfriend Angie in the Park Service Employee Housing at Lodgepole, making the hour and forty-five minute drive in my yellow 1972 Toyota Corolla, a car my dad loaned me the money to buy so I would have something reliable for the commute.

Eight hours of class at the school, a ten minute drive to the KOA, clean up in coin-operated showers at the campground, eat dinner out of a can, study my books and notes by a kerosene lamp, sleep fitfully in the narrow bed and rise to another day of the same. Sometimes at night the KOA would have loud groups of rowdy bikers or other strangers. Members of the central valley chapter of the outlaw Mongols Motorcycle Club were known to hold gatherings there. I kept the flimsy door latched from the inside. This had been my life for six weeks. It was lonely and often scary. I didn't know it yet but it would be a forerunner of my life as a construction worker.

My shoe is glowing cherry-red now. I tong it out and lay it on the anvil with a little ringing sound. Picking up my two-pound rounding hammer, I begin to beat on the hot steel with light pushing blows, moving the molten metal outwards, flattening it, rounding it, building with hammer strokes the paddle-shaped heels which would allow a horse to rock back and slide in soft arena dirt. Before the metal cools to black, I poke it back into the fire.

Building a horseshoe is kind of like writing a story, you have to hammer it into shape with a lot of little taps, pushing it this way and that way until it shapes up into something useable. When I was little, my dad used to bring me piles of paper from work. He would use the big paper-cutter at his office to cut up old blueprints. A little red stapler and the piles of cut-up blueprints became my fodder.

When I was as young as seven I would get up early in the morning and sit on the bottom step of the staircase that went up to the second story bedroom I shared with Elly. With a heat register blowing warmed air up between my socked feet, I would sit on that step and write stories on the back of the blueprint papers, staple them together, use my crayons to illustrate them, and when I had a little stack of stories, I'd run into the kitchen where my father would be sitting reading the newspaper, drinking his coffee. I would climb into his lap and read my stories to him. That was something we had always shared, my dad and me, the desire to be a writer.

He was a city planner who wanted to be Hemingway. He looked like Papa from his late forties on, as his hair and beard went from dark to steel-gray to silver to white. When he was living in San Francisco and I was living in San Francisco working at the police stable, I used to spend each Thursday night at his tiny basement apartment on Page Street next door to the Park Branch Library, having dinner with him and his lady friend "Mac" Klarich, talking about writing. I would read to him from my latest novel in progress, he would read to me from one of his many unfinished stories. He was my most constructive critic and a creative and unorthodox thinker.

Pop was the sort of person who, if he went to the big St. Patrick's Day parade, he would spend more time watching the people than the parade. Later he wouldn't be able to remember a single float but, man, he could recount in minute detail the characters he saw in the crowd!

If someone gave him a straw Fedora for Christmas wrapped up in bright tissue paper and ribbons to disguise its shape, he'd feel the package until he discovered what it was, punch a hole in the bottom of the wrapping and put it on his head, tissue paper, ribbons and all. He would wear the hat like that for weeks, to his doctor appointments, on the bus, on his rounds in the Haight-Ashbury. "What's with the hat,

Ed?" neighbors, shopkeepers and homeless guys would ask. "I got it for Christmas," my dad would say. "Ain't it marvelous?" He'd wear the hat until the decorations faded and the wrapping paper wore away and the hat returned to its original mundane parameters. And then he'd continue to wear it as a kind of memorial to its former glory.

The tongs were in my hand. I was gazing deep into the glowing fire, where the black outline of my sliding plate was fading into white. The ringing of hammers on anvils had lulled me into a dreamlike state. I reached in and grasped my shoe with the tongs and pulled it out. It was white-hot and sparking. I laid it on the anvil and watched as the edges of the curved steel popped and flared, sending tiny fireworks in the air. It ticked as it cooled slowly to cherry-red and I could see the edges were uneven, nibbled away by the intense heat of the fire.

Shit! I had cooked my sliding plate!

With disgust, I flung the ruined shoe into the water bucket with a loud Hiss!

The burnt hunk of iron sank to the bottom of the dingy water and lay there. Now I would have to start all over again. I turned and stared into the maw of the coal forge. The inferno within roiled like a volcano's innards, white hot, roaring, stinging the skin of my cheeks, sucking at my hair. It reminded me of the great stump holes I had seen on the mountain last summer from under my fire-fighter's hard hat. And of great trees crumbling into ash sending up geysers of sparks and embers. And of the most amazing thing I had ever seen.

It made me wonder if I ever told my dad about...

12

The Flaming Arrow
In which I tell my dad a story I never told him

Pop, did I ever tell you the story of the flaming arrow?

You weren't feeling very good last summer (now we know it was your heart) and I was busy at Sequoia working so I didn't get up to visit much. It was the day I passed my step test and received my red card, the certification of my completion of the Fire Science course. I was now a member of the Lodgepole Emergency Fire-fighting crew! My new crew-mates were wrapping up a prescribed burn in the Giant Forest area of Sequoia National Park and my crew chief, Trey, said, "Jump in the truck, I'll take you out with me to monitor the burn."

I was eager to go, even though I wasn't on payroll yet. We drove for a while and then saw the smoke. Soon, we had burnt forest on our left and we turned off the General's Highway right after the old cafeteria, since removed. Nomex-clad fire-fighters with McLeod and Pulaski in hand were working the fire-line as we drove down the Moro Rock/Crescent Meadow road. They raised their gloved hands and waved as we motored by.

"You want to see something very few people in the history of the world have ever seen?" Trey said, as he pulled over near the Tunnel Log, an ancient fallen Sequoia with a hole notched out of it for cars to drive through.

"Well, yeah," I said. Like, who wouldn't?

Trey got out and crammed his hard hat on his head. He grabbed a McLeod out of the truck-bed. "Follow me," he said, mysteriously. I put on my own helmet and followed him. We picked up the Soldier's Trail, which had been used as the easternmost fire-line of the prescribed burn. We were in dense forest dominated by towering red-barked Sequoia Gigantia, each of which had a circular fire-line cut around it for protection of this endangered species. The understory was Douglas Fir, white and red fir, various types of pines and shrubs. To our left as we walked down the trail was "the black," or burned-out part of the forest with the understory trees charred and smoking, the ground cover reduced to warm gray ash. On the right the forest was lush, green and solidly packed with vegetation.

A quarter-mile down the trail, Trey stopped abruptly. "Do you hear it?" I listened intently and then I did hear something. A faint whistle in the distance, like a steam engine. Trey smiled when he saw the change on my face. "You won't believe this," he said, turning on his heel and bouncing on down the trail. I jogged after him, following his muscular form as his long legs ate up the next quarter-mile. The sound grew louder, resolving itself from a whistle to a roar. A patch of white-thorn to the right side blocked my view until we rounded it and the trail straightened. "There it is!" Trey cried exultantly.

I looked ahead and was unsure for a moment exactly what I was looking at. The roar was so loud it was hard to hear Trey speak. "The fir tree next to it," he was saying, pointing to a blackened snag, "caught fire and the fire burned out to the end of one of its larger branches. That branch transferred fire to one of the lower branches of the Sequoia and the Sequoia branch burned all the way to the trunk." I knew that a Sequoia tree's twelve-inch-plus thick bark is virtually fireproof. Most of the Sequoias that have caught fire over the long centuries have only caught fire because the protective bark was in some way breached and the fire enabled to gain access to the flammable heartwood. Even so, many of the Big Trees that show extensive fire damage still live, growing scar tissue over the burned areas in nature's effort to protect the exposed and vulnerable interior. A short hike along the Congress Trail in the Giant Forest presents to the visitor several examples of Sequoias that have survived devastating forest fires and lived to see many more centuries of life.

Trey was continuing. "Then the Sequoia branch burned through the bark to the inside of the tree." Now, suddenly, I realized what I was seeing. I raised my head, casting my gaze up the unblemished red shaggy bark of the large Sequoia next to the blackened snag of the fir tree. Twenty-five feet above the ground was a hole in the side of the Sequoia, a circular hole about five feet in diameter. "The embers burned straight through to the heartwood and it began to burn," Trey was saying. "After a couple of days, it has completely hollowed out the trunk and the fire has climbed to the top."

I tipped my head back further to look at the top of the Big Tree, some two hundred feet above me. A column of dark smoke boiled out of the top as if it were coming out of a smoke stack. "The tree has become a living chimney," Trey concluded.

"Unbelieveable!" was all I could find to say.

"Believe it," Trey said. "It's right before your eyes."

I thought of the trees on the Congress Trail where I had hiked so many times. One of them was called the Spyglass Tree and if you stood inside its hollowed-out base and looked straight up, you could see out the top of it to the open sky. A long-ago fire had hollowed it out. How long ago? Hundreds of years? A thousand? Now, here I was, witnessing the same thing happening to another tree. Like Trey had said, seeing a sight that few human beings in the world had ever seen. And probably, very few living ones. I looked at my crew boss with gratitude. "God, Trey," I gushed, "thanks for bringing me out here!"

He smiled smugly. "I had a feeling you'd appreciate it, Amy."

"I do," I said, taking a couple steps towards the tree.

"Don't go too close," Trey admonished.

My natural curiosity was piqued, however. I wanted to see inside the trunk, see the actual fire, not just hear the roar and see the smoke. "I won't," I assured him, though I knew I was lying. I was gonna get as close as the heat would allow me!

And the heat was intense! I turned one shoulder towards it as I approached the base of the Sequoia, stepping over the charred ground and gray heaps of ash. The roar got louder the closer I got. It was the roar not so much of fire but of wind. I could feel the wind rushing by me as the fire sucked the air into the hollow trunk, consumed the oxygen from it, and pumped the rest of it with the ash and smoke out the top of the tree. All around me, the ground was littered with large red-hot embers that broke loose from inside and pin-balled down and out the hole. I had to be careful they didn't land in my clothes. One bounced and landed at my feet as I craned my neck to see inside. "That's close enough!" I heard Trey yell, barely audible in the roar.

My eyes watered from the heat and I squinted them almost closed. My left cheek burned where I had it turned towards the fire. The hair from my braid was getting pulled out and sucked towards the tree. My clothing flapped. But I could see!

Up inside the hole was a red-orange glow. It was like looking into a volcano. I blinked my eyes and looked again, trying to focus. The inferno within resolved itself into individual embers, some orange, some red, bright yellow and white. Wriggling lines of flames undulated over the entire surface, traveling upwards in a twisting intricate dance, and tiny blue flares flashed up and died. There was a whining, sizzling, whistling, sucking, thrumming roar against my eardrums. And occasional great explosive pops and hisses.

"Come on back, Amy!" Trey shouted through cupped hands as several fresh embers pinged out of the opening and shot past me. I retreated quickly, my flesh prickling with the heat. "You should see that!" I enthused when I had joined Trey back on the trail.

Trey shook his head. "You're lucky you didn't burn up," he said. I wondered if he was going to throw me off the fire crew for reckless behavior, a thing we had been schooled against in training. I tried to hang my head and look contrite but he could still see the excited gleam in my eyes. "Chance of a lifetime," I murmured. "I think I would have kicked myself if I passed up the chance to see that."

"I know," the crew boss said. "I have to admit, I did it too, last time I was out here." He winked at me. "Don't tell my boss."

We stood for a while, admiring the burning Sequoia. Trey reached in his back pocket and pulled forth a tin of Copenhagen, ducking a dip into his lower lip. I smelled the minty scent.

"Will it live, do you think?" I asked, thinking of the Spyglass, a living example of such a wonder as I was now witnessing.

"I hope so," he said. "The point of these prescribed burns is to protect the Sequoias in the long term by burning the understory out in a controlled fashion so that some wildfire can't blast through here so hot that the Big Trees catch fire, and also to prepare the soil for Sequoia seeds to actually grow into full-size trees, something that hasn't happened much since man started preventing forest fires. Fire actually helps dry out the Sequoia cones and releases the seed onto the newly-cleared ground." Trey shook his head, marveling. "Nature's perfect plan. Come back here in a year or two and you'll be amazed at the numbers of tiny baby Sequoia trees that will be growing in here."

"What about the risk to the grown trees, though?" I asked, remembering my Fire Science class. "I mean, the fire jumps the lines sometimes, doesn't it?"

He shrugged. "We do what we can to keep them from catching fire in prescribed burns but it still happens, rarely. But on the other hand, this situation here is a perfect example of why we burn. In a natural state, that fir tree that caught the Sequoia on fire would not have even been there, it probably would have burned up in a previous fire before it got to the size where it could threaten the Big Tree. Being pitchy, firs and pines are far more flammable than Sequoias. When they catch fire, it is like having a bunch of hot flaming torches in the Sequoia forest, very dangerous for the Sequoias."

I nodded, getting the picture. "Well, I hope the Sequoia makes it." Trey let fly a squirt of tobacco juice onto the ground. "These trees are very resilient. This one is on relatively flat ground and it's still got about twenty-five feet of a good solid unburned base. That bottom will act like a pedestal for the hollowed-out trunk to stand on. Only the outer layer, just under the bark, called the cambium, is actually living tissue. The heartwood, the entire interior, is non-living and simply provides support." Trey removed his hard hat and wiped a hand across his sweaty brow, raking his fingers through his wet dark curls. "It's got a good chance of surviving this fire and living long after you and me and everyone we know, and probably even our grandkids, are dead, gone and forgotten." He smiled at me.

"That's totally cool," I said. Cool was a better word for the moment than profound, but profound was what I was thinking.

"We're calling it the Flaming Arrow," he said, "because just down that way," he pointed down the trail, "is the Broken Arrow, a burned Sequoia snag that John Muir himself named. A tree that, unlike this one, did not survive its fire. Do you want to go see it?"

"Sure," I said, "I'd like to see something that John Muir named."

Trey put on his helmet and led the way, off trail into the green, the unburned part of the forest. Standing in the center of a clearing, the Broken Arrow looked like a New Age sculpture constructed of charred wood black as a raven's wing, narrow at the base and broadening out to look like an arrowhead pointed at the sky. Its abstract form was stark and interesting against the verdant hues of the forest. It towered above me and I walked around it, gazing up, admiring its flowing flanks and sharp angles, all carved by the natural impulses of fire. I thought Pop would love to see this sculpture!

To Trey, I said, "Wow, it looks like it could fall at any moment."

"Yet it has stood like that only God knows how many centuries," the crew boss said. "At least since Muir's time and probably a lot longer."

"A heavy snow could topple it," I observed.

"And probably will," Trey agreed. "One day. We better get back. I have to check in with the crew on the west line." We walked back to the truck, pausing just a couple minutes at the Flaming Arrow to fix it in our minds. It was a sight I would never forget.

So Pop, did I never tell you the story of the Flaming Arrow?

I hope you're listening.

13

The White Bird
In which I bid my father farewell

Out of the darkness, a great white bird swoops low and almost strikes the windshield of my Corolla as I drive along Highway 190. The headlights illuminate the fluffy white breast feathers of the bird as it beats its long wings once, twice, slowly gaining altitude, bwanging my car's antenna as it barely clears.

"What the hell?" I say aloud. I am a little drunk and probably shouldn't be driving at all, but that has nothing to do with almost hitting the white bird. What the hell was an egret doing flying around at night anyway?

I have just left the party at John Bozanich's ranch in Springville. John is one of the students in my class at the horseshoeing school and he and his wife had hosted our midterm exam party, with a traditional cowboy tri-tip barbecue and ice chests full of beer. I had passed the written test with the flying colors my dad had predicted and spent the afternoon building shoes and shoeing my half a horse, taking turns with Cliff, a ruddy tobacco-spitting cowboy from Montana.

The chestnut mare we drew was calm and gentle and I had done well, with the exception of having let the rasp cut a little too deeply into the medial quarter of the right front, leaving a gap between hoof and shoe that Mr. Newmar quickly spotted even though I had tried to rub dirt over it so it wouldn't be obvious. A mistake that amounted to nothing more than a cosmetic flaw and was something upon which I would improve with experience. I had hardly had time to think about my dad all day, knowing he had been prepped for surgery early in the morning and would probably be in recovery most of the afternoon. I kept my mind on my work and when the exam was done, I caravanned with the other students up to Boz's place for the party.

Stuffing myself on macaroni and potato salad and bread and butter (being a vegetarian since age 13, I couldn't eat the meat or the beans which were cooked with a big ham-hock), I drank a few beers and danced with Sally to the George Strait music that played on the sound system. At about 10:30 pm, I said my good-byes and got into my little car to drive back to the KOA.

It is then I see the white bird. A night-flying egret which damned near smashes itself against my windshield. A jolt of adrenaline sings through my veins as the bird appears and disappears and my hands start to shake on the steering wheel. I suddenly have a very bad feeling. I haven't called anyone to find out how my dad is. I've gone all day without hearing anything and then I had rushed off to a party without calling my mom or my sister Susan or anyone.

Now a white bird. Where (or when) one should not be.

Among Native American tribes the untimely sighting of a white bird presages death. My hands are shaking when I turn into the campground and bump down the dirt road. As my headlights settle on my trailer, I notice Angie's truck pulled up alongside of it. This had never happened before, my girlfriend driving down the mountain at night to join me in my trailer. Angie is leaning against the hood of the Toyota pickup, her coat collar pulled up around her neck, her hands in her pockets.

I park and get out. "Wow, what are you doing here?" I call, walking towards her for a hug.

The look on her face stops me.

"Honey, it's your dad."

"My dad?" I say. "What happened?"

"It's not good."

Then it hits home, my dad's surgery has not gone well. My dad is in trouble, maybe my dad is going to die. I had better get up to San Francisco. I run for the trailer door, flipping through my keys for the right one. A horrible feeling has gripped me, worse than fear, a terrible sickening guilt that I hadn't really thought of Pop all day, so caught up in my own stuff had I been! If I had been paying attention... but of course that was crazy, I couldn't have influenced a surgical operation, one way or the other. But that was behind now, what mattered now was that I go to him. See him, hold his hand. If he was going to die, tell him I love him. As many times as I could. "I'll pack!" I say to Angie over my shoulder. "I'll be ready to leave in a minute!"

"Wait," she says. She follows me to the trailer and puts a hand on my shoulder as I find the right key and undo the lock.

"I'll be ready in a minute!" I say again. "Then we can leave to go see my dad!"

"Amy," she says and her voice breaks. "It's... too late. It's too late to see him."

I turn and look at her. Her face is wet with tears. "Susan called me, hours ago. I tried calling the school. No one answered. I remembered you guys had a party planned but I didn't know where. All I could do is come here and wait for you."

"But, my dad..."

"Amy, he's gone. He's dead."

"Oh, God," I say, before I begin to cry.

"Let's go inside and turn on the heater," Angie says. "We'll leave in the morning."

The family gathers at my mom's Mill Valley home, the barn-shaped house next door to Boyle Park with the little bridge over the creek in front, the house which, upon buying it in 1964, my parents had christened The House Of Love And Joy: My mother, Jody, besides being a mother of seven, is the founding director of an outpatient day-care center for adults with mental disorders; my sister Susan, a marriage and family counselor (later PhD); brother Steve, a computer engineer working for Sun Microsystems; my sister Elly, world traveler and private home-care nurse; brother Andy, a student at Cal Poly San Luis Obispo; brother Peter, at the time a rebellious and troubled young man; and the youngest, sister Felicia, who is still in high school.

The operation, Susan reports, had taken much longer than the team of doctors had anticipated. The massive amounts of scar tissue left over from Dad's first open heart surgery in 1974 had made cutting open the chest difficult and closing tricky. They had accomplished the task but taken double the average time and when they tried to get the heart to take over from the blood pump, the heart was unresponsive. My father had signed a living will the day before that clearly stated no heroics, and so after advising Susan, the machines had been turned off.

It was that simple. The operation had been a success but the patient had died. It was the kind of gallows humor my dad would've loved. As per his final wishes, his body would be cremated and the ashes relinquished to the family. Before that happened, we were to view the body at Russell and Gooch's Funeral home in Mill Valley, no frills, no dressed-up oversize doll in the casket, no candles burning, no chapel with music playing. No, that was not Ed Farrell's way. We were to see death without all the velvet plush to dull the blow.

It was a little too stark for some of us. But the way Pop had seen it, the less money spent on what was done with his dead body the more money there would be to do something useful with. We sit in the lobby of the funeral home and take turns by twos and threes going into the preparation room to see the remains. The room is a laboratory, white-walled and stainless steeled, with trays of instruments and tanks of embalming fluids, a drain in the center of the floor. Pop lies under bright florescent lights, a white sheet pulled up under his chin, snowy white beard combed neatly and hair arranged in a style he had never worn it in life. Elly on one side of me and Steve on the other both utter strangled cries.

I walk across the room and gaze down at the still gray face.

The familiar seams and features are all there but it looks like someone's bad wax model molded to certain parameters but lacking the artistic depth to create a convincing likeness. I lay my hands on my father's chest and hear the crackle of plastic under the sheet. Pulling the white sheet back, I find that the body, nude, is wrapped in plastic sheeting like a great plucked chicken in a grocer's freezer. I tuck the sheet back under the clenched jaw, noticing a deep purple layer in the flesh of the neck where the blood has settled towards the gurney on which the body lies. Blood pooled in tissue, pulled only by the force of gravity. Blood unmoved by the great heart now stilled, a heart which had beat, keeping time as in a piece of music which played without cease, for sixty-three years.

I look down at the composed face and see not my father there, the monolithic individual whose principles and passions had informed my own, who had been an archetype for me of evolving Man, battling base nature while constantly struggling to refine the higher impulses, a powerful personality with great intuition and creativity but yet with a rational and analytical mind, a mover and shaker who dominated any gathering with sheer force of presence, an ideas man whose mind was never at rest, a spark, a firebrand, a raging inferno of mental and emotional energy. No, I see not my father here, in this still cold mound of flesh. The man I loved is gone from here and this remnant is but a sorry byproduct of an enterprise that had been both grand and presumptive.

Death, I see, is a slap to the face of the ego. So much went into the making of a human being like Ed Farrell: Sired by man and born of woman with all the components for greatness or failure inherent unto himself; sparking white-hot in the fire of his own desires, dreams and follies; worked and reworked by his own hand on the anvil of life into a cohesive and useful form, a unique expression of the will of God. At once, a beautiful and terrible expression of the universe.

Death, what an insult! We are All That, and when we die, Nothing. A lump of ill-shaped modeling clay. As if what we are, and do, matters not at all. So, I do not see my father there, or rather what I see is not his passion and his struggle, that has gone, like a fiery arrow shot to the sky. What is left is in stillness, whereas he had never been so. What had been his fire, his glory and his torment, now is free. Left behind is only that which had hindered him.

I hear my brother's cry and my sister's sobs. I have hot tears streaking down my face but my mind is not in anguish. "He's all right," I say, my hands upon the still chest.

"He's not all right," Steve croaks.

"Yes, you see, he is all right now."

"He's dead," my brother cries.

I glance at him. Steve's handsome face is wet with tears and twisted with grief. His trim muscular body arches and bends in upon itself, folding his 6' 4" frame like a book being closed. The angles of his chiseled cheeks are sharp, almost skeletal, as his teeth clamp shut, holding his cries inside. He wrings his hands and steps from foot to foot as if looking for escape.

There are pictures, old black and whites, of my father at Steve's age; tall, lean and handsome, narrow-hipped and broad-shouldered, white shirt sleeves rolled up for a task at hand, his hair rakishly swept back from a smooth wide forehead. While Steve's hair is red and his lip bears a neat mustache where my father in his youth had been clean shaven, the resemblance is clear. Of three boys, Steve is the only natural born son of my parents and so, of all of us, bears the most likeness. Perhaps he sees himself upon that gurney.

Elly cries in sympathy and goes to hold him in her arms. They weep together and then, with Elly's gentle urging, come to stand beside me near our father's body. We link arms and hold a silent vigil for long moments, our tears running from our chins and falling onto the crisp white sheet. Beside me, Steve's body shakes with grief. From his other side, Elly's hand reaches behind our brother and finds my hand and squeezes it hard.

"He didn't want to be dead," Steve wails.

"He's all right now," I repeat. I don't know why I feel this, or how I know this, but I feel a stillness in my heart which so radically juxtaposes my brother's panic. It is as if I know that all my father's yearning, craving, reaching, grasping, searching, thirsting, never-satisfied nature is now somehow sated. No, he hadn't wanted to be dead. There were things, oh, many things left undone, many plans uncompleted, many ideas unexplored, many wild hares unchased. He hadn't wanted to be dead, but now somehow, he is all right with it. He has moved on to something else of interest.

A child raised without religion, I don't know why I have always had some inexplicable faith that there is something after death, some new life we go to. Though my father did not believe this, I believe it now for him. Or perhaps I believe it now for me, perhaps it is the only way to get through this experience unscathed. Perhaps my calm assurance is purely selfish, a mechanism for survival.

Steve's feet cannot hold him in this room any longer. He wipes his face, paces up and down once like a caged panther, and leaves. Elly and I share another minute. She is a nurse and I am curious by nature. She watches as I pull up the sheet and examine our father's body, as much as can be seen through the plastic wrap. The incision in his chest. The toes of his feet, with the heavy yellow horny nails, bearing a tag with his name.

FARRELL, ED.

"The Ecstatic Dancer," I say and we smile. As a writing byline, Pop had often used the acronym E. D. for "Ecstatic Dancer," a reference to his wild, exuberant and insatiable zest for life. It was his name for himself, the name he felt summed him up best. But Elly and I know, the still lifeless form under the white sheet is not the Ecstatic Dancer.

The Ecstatic Dancer has gone.

Amy R Farrell

14

Don't Wait For Life
In which I help my brother die and he helps me to live

Four years later, I lay with my brother Steve in his deathbed, holding his skeletal form in my strong construction worker arms. My five foot six inches besides his six-four, we shared one bed each night and through much of the day, laying in an intimacy almost like lovers. He sick and I well, he weak and I strong, he barely able to raise and I able to bound up and fetch at a moment's need. His once beautiful body, ravaged by AIDS, had winnowed down to angular bone and thin skin. His big blue eyes gazed out from a skull-like face, lovely in its stark simplicity. Caring for my dying brother was a privilege, sharing his bed to better hear and serve his minute needs. His voice was a ragged thread of a whisper and a whisper in the night is best heard with an ear in near proximity. "Help me to roll on my side."

"Can you get me a drink of water?"

"Can you move my arm from under me?"

A whisper during the day is best heard by an ear close by. "Sis, could you help me to eat this soup?"

"My friend is visiting today. Can you help me sit up, dress and shave?"

Perhaps my brother had seen himself in the man on the gurney at Russell and Gooch's Funeral Home. He would lay there soon enough himself, although we would come see Steve in the chapel, with the velvet plush, the candles and the soft light, the soothing music and the flowers. Sharing his deathbed with him for those days so nigh to his final ones, I saw that his mortal panic had by then relaxed into a gentle skepticism or, perhaps, better said, a humorous philosophical-ness.

"Shit happens," he said to me with the ghost of a laugh. "Sometimes it happens to me."

My brother Steve was ever a thoughtful man, with his own sagacity and wisdom, a man about whom it could not be said that he waltzed through life without ever looking around him, and as, at age 38, he approached his death, it seemed he took the time remaining to reexamine life and to impart to the people around him those things he found important for a living person to remember.

"Don't wait for life," he said to me one afternoon as the San Francisco sun streamed through the mullioned window and warmed the feather comforter on the cherry-wood bed that was now the solitary continent of his once wide world. "There is so much I wanted yet to do," he said. "So you must promise me, that you will go out and do the things you dream of. Don't wait for life. It may get away from you."

More than twenty years later, I write this. Realizing as I write that I have indeed waited for life. That I have risked letting it get away from me. The novels uncompleted, the books unpublished, the reams of poems, short stories and tales unshared with any but my closest circle.

"Don't wait for life," my brother had said.

"Write a book about it, Kiddo," the Ecstatic Dancer had told me I when I was just a child.

"Write a book and give it to the world."

PART THREE:

MINOTAURS AND MEN

I believe a strong woman may be stronger than a man, particularly if she happens to have love in her heart.

-John Steinbeck, East Of Eden

15

Alkali Flats and Blazing Shovels
In which I break ground at Corcoran State Prison

"**So** this is Corcoran," I said to myself, approving whole-heartedly of the great State of California's choice of location for the next State Penitentiary. "What a hell hole." Crossing a number of railroad tracks and driving my old truck down the main street of the almost abandoned little town, I glanced right and left at boarded-up storefronts and dodged potholes big enough to swallow me, seeing no one but a hobo pushing a laden shopping cart with a crooked wheel down the sidewalk.

I took another look at the scrap of paper on which I had written the directions to the job site that Darce Daniels had given me on the phone when he had called the previous evening at 7 p.m. to dispatch me to this job. "Ah gots a job fer ya," he had said, in his Ditchbank Okie drawl, just as I was sitting down for dinner.

"Really?" I had said, both glad and disappointed. "Where at?" Glad for the money I would make, disappointed that my plans to ride my horse Dreamer to the base of Coomb Rocks the next day were shot.

"Th' new fed'ral prison et Corcoran. Ya know wee-r it is?"

"No, sir," I had said, grabbing a pencil and piece of paper.

Darce gave me the directions and said, "Start tam 7 ayem. Comp'ny outta Baaaykersfield, call't WDI. Don't be late, gurl. Thay'll have yer skinny little ay-ss outa there inna heartbate. Long drave fer nuthin.'"

"Yes, sir."

Now here it was a quarter to seven. I was driving through this po-dunk burg looking for Chambers Road, upon which a left turn was supposed to take me straight to the job site. I had risen at 4 o'clock, left at five, given myself two hours to get here but now I was thinking it was maybe not enough. Damn it!

Cursing like a mule-skinner who'd done a couple years as a longshoreman and was afflicted with Turrette's Syndrome, I crumpled the piece of paper and threw it onto the floor boards. I was already at the outskirts of town and I had not seen Chambers. I could turn around and run it again, or... no, I kept on going. The prison wouldn't be being built close to the town, it would be out in the boonies.

It was nothing but flat land in all directions, an expanse of dry white dusty alkali flats for miles around. Perfect spot for a prison! At not yet seven in the morning it was already 79 degrees. With no air conditioning in my truck, both windows rolled down, I was wet with sweat.

I glared into the early morning sun and saw what I was looking for! The tall silhouette of an excavator on the horizon. I found a road and drove towards it. As I came abreast of the machine but still about a mile away, I selected a rutted dirt road which ran in the machine's general direction. A rooster tail of white powdery dust flaring off behind me, I jounced as fast as I could down the road. I had to make several other direction changes, finally giving up on the dirt roads entirely and heading across uncharted territory, before I came up to the excavator. Men in dirty work clothes were standing about in the usual pre-work coffee klatch (sans campfire) as I drove up, my white dust cloud blowing over them, adding another layer of dirt to that already on them.

"WDI?" I hollered out of my truck window.

"No, Smith and Walermann."

"Know where WDI is?"

The men shaded their eyes against the dust and sun glare. One of them pointed west into a broad expanse of nothingness. "Over that way, I think."

"Thanks," I said glancing at my watch.

Six-fifty-six. Shit! Or as Darce would say, Sheee-it on a steee-ick! I raised a fresh cloud of dust as I raced off, not even looking for a trail or track across the white soil, just hauling ass across the desert-like terrain. Dodging the occasional low bush and bumping my poor little truck into an occasional depression and bouncing back out of it, I made my way west until I spotted a Seatrain shipping container and headed for it.

I parked next to the huge battered metal box and got out of the truck, grabbing my hard hat and gloves. There was a trailer next to the Seatrain, the kind companies often set up on job sites for use as an office or headquarters. Other than that, there were some bundles of re-enforcing steel (rebar) bent into different configurations, some drums of wax emulsion and form release, and a small dumpster. I walked around the Seatrain and past the dumpster on my left. Suddenly there was a horrible growl and a dark form leapt almost on top of me from the dumpster. I jumped back, my heart in my mouth.

A large black dog with patches of raw skin exposed through mangy fur landed at my feet, snarled and slunk away, a greasy paper sack in its jaws. My pulse was racing as I watched the dog run off over the barren ground with its prize.

Turning, I continued my search for my new employers. Past the office trailer the ground suddenly dropped away into a huge excavation, about twenty feet deep and about two thirds the size of a football field. There was a kind of ramp dug into the soil for people and equipment to access the bottom. A Caterpillar 245 excavator, a front loader, several dump trucks and various other "iron" was parked in the hole and a group of men was standing near the Cat. I ran down the ramp to join them, raising another, smaller, cloud of dust. "WDI?" I called as I neared them, hoping it was and that I didn't have to run back to my truck and make another mad dash across the alkali flats looking for another company.

"WDI," a heavyset man affirmed. "Local 294?'

"That's right, I'm Amy," I said, shaking his hand.

"Bernie," he said, "I'm the job superintendent. Come up to the trailer real quick, Amy. I've got some papers for you to sign." We started walking back up the ramp. Bernie was heavy and didn't walk real well on the uneven ground. Not only was the excavated soil lumpy, it was powdery. Our feet sank into the surface about 6 inches, poofing as if they were entering a layer of finely ground flour, little jets of dust being propelled skyward and coating our pants up to the knees. We had to step higher than normal to pull our feet clear of the stuff and make the next stride. Each step was accompanied by a little suffing sound as the foot was raised out of the powder and the powder fell back into the hole it left. Bernie was panting hard and sweating profusely by the time we got to the office. His khaki chinos were white from the knee down and I could not tell what color his boots were supposed to be.

He glanced at the thermometer next to the door. "Only seven-oh-five and its fuckin' hot as a Nevada whorehouse in July," he muttered as he held the door for me, "and its only God damn March!"

The air-conditioning inside was like a blast of refrigerated air. The sweat had dried on me by the time I signed my papers and got up to leave. My skin already had a fine layer of white dust on it and I hadn't even started work. "What're we building here, Bernie?" I asked, my hand on the door latch.

"Sewer plant for the prison," he said. "Just report to Russ, he's in charge of the shovel jockeys."

"Thank you, sir."

"And kid?"

"Yes, sir?"

"I hope you can handle the heat, 'cause it's gonna be a hell of a job and we're in a hurry."

The white alkali flats in the area of Corcoran, CA are all that remains of the old Tulare Lake, the largest fresh water body in the Western United States, which was systematically drained in the late 19th century to make way for farming. The snowmelt-fed rivers which course down the western slopes of the Sierra Nevada dump unceremoniously into the San Joaquin Valley, creating a series of deltas, creeks, streams, swamps, and one great shallow lake, the Tulare, approximately 570 square miles of it! Before the age of civilization, these wild waterways fed a fertile landscape of wet grasslands which hosted an abundance of wildlife. Large herbivores such as elk, moose and deer abounded, along with carnivores including grizzly bear. Huge flocks of water birds, ducks, geese, herons, egrets and pelicans made their living on the waterways and in the Tulare Lake, feasting on fish, shell fish and frogs.

In the mid to late 1800s, white settlers established fisheries on the waters of Tulare Lake and simultaneously began hunting the birds for their feathers, supplying the milliners' trade back east. Eventually, as the area was populated and developed, towns established and railroads built, the waterways were corralled into irrigation canals and channeled purposefully to farms and businesses. The rivers, the Kings, the Kaweah and the Tule, were dammed and large reservoirs created. The great Tulare Lake was drained, much of the land used for farming, and some of it in western Tulare County and eastern Kings County left barren, a dry white arid expanse.

Periodically, in years of heavy rainfall, this area floods, reverting temporarily to a semblance of its former self. Water birds still visit the area on their yearly migration patterns, including the ungainly white pelicans, which look out of place in this inland "desert." Great blue herons and egrets, which look more at home in swamps and marshes, still ply their fishing trade along the man-made canals and ditches, and are often seen in newly-plowed fields catching gophers with their long pointed bills. The powdery white-ish soil of the old Tulare Lake still contains the bleached shells of fresh water shellfish. I still have a freshwater clamshell I found while pushing a muck-stick on that job. The thing measures four and a half inches across!

The first weeks of the project were spent building a huge French drain underneath what would become the concrete sewer ponds. I laid thousands of square feet of black filter fabric, spread on a layer of 2 inch drain rock (or round gravel), assembled 8 inch perforated drain pipe in a grid pattern on top of that and covered with another layer of drain rock. All the while sump pumps were running to keep the hole from flooding because the water table is extremely high out in the lake bottom. These pumps ran 24 hours a day. When they happened to quit during the night, our work site would be underwater by morning.

The handful of other shovel jockeys and I pushed a lot of rock creating that pad! Two-inch drain rock doesn't exactly flow into the muck-stick like sifted fine dirt does, or even 3/4 inch crushed gravel. My arms ached with the jarring effort of slamming a shovel into the rock and heft-hefting it to make the rock jump into the shovel, then lifting the loaded shovel and flinging the rock where it was needed. The noise of half a dozen muck-sticks assaulting rock was deafening, added to the din of diesel-powered machines bringing us more rock and dumping heaps over the drain pipe, pinging and clattering over the PVC. The dust rose in clouds for us to breathe. The heat in the bottom of that hole, where no breezes ever reached, and the sun reflecting off of the white walls of the excavation, was intense, akin to working inside a solar oven.

It was early in March 1987 and we had broken ground on the Corcoran Prison project, where, sometime in the future, the infamous megalomaniac and messiah to murderers, Charles Manson, would be incarcerated, serving out his life sentence without parole. The run-down little railroad town of Corcoran, California would experience a huge economic boost and within ten years would undergo a huge face-lift and see a major improvement in quality of life.

I was to work there through the spring of that year and one of the hottest summers on record for the great central valley of California.

16

Corcoran Prison Blues
In which I suffer the slings and arrows of ironworker incorrigibility

"**Hey**, you!" one of the ironworkers yelled at me.

I looked up from picking up a load of steel construction stakes. Balancing the heavy stakes on my shoulder, I squinted at the guy in the bright sun of the alkali flats. "Whatja want?" I hollered. The stakes were hot from the sun and one of them was burning my neck where it rested against my skin.

"Well, fuck me!" the man said. "I thought somebody'd brought their little girl out here fer Father-daughter-go-to-work Day, but fuck me if you don't think you're a laborer! We gotta name fer girls like you!"

I nodded, playing along. "What name would that be?" I hollered back, thinking of one of my mantras, "Take it like a duck." It was best to just let these guys be assholes and let them see that you could handle it right off the bat. They usually toned it down after the first day or so. This guy was new on the job. The ironworkers had just arrived to begin building the steel re-enforcing for the slab floor of the sewer plant's immense water storage ponds, which would be three solid feet of steel-re-enforced concrete.

After we laborers had completed the French drain, a crew of carpenters had arrived. Working under a carpenter foreman from WDI called Clint, we proceeded to form an oval shape on the bottom of the hole the approximate shape of a football field only in about 2/3 the scale. Using batter boards and string-lines, the "termites," as carpenters are known, had taught me how an immense structure like this is laid out. I had driven hundreds of long steel construction stakes with a 10 pound sledge-hammer and nailed 3 x 8 foot sheets of plywood to the stakes, setting duplex nails in the holes in the stakes and knocking them through the wood with a 20-oz Estwing hammer. We set kicker stakes on the diagonal deep into the ground and nailed off to the form wood to give the forms support when the wet cement was poured and vibrated into place.

Now that the oval was formed, it was time for the ironworkers to lay three tiers of elaborate steel rebar matting. About twenty of these "rodbusters" had blown in this morning, acting like they owned the place. Rodbusters have the foulest mouths of any construction workers I know (with the possible exception of hard-rock miners), and they swagger around as if they have balls as big as a bull's. The cock-swinging commandos of construction, they lord it over every other male on the site. Now I was going to see how they treated the only female.

"What name is that?" I hollered at the ironworker.

He laughed, showing two broken teeth in his lower jaw. "You really wanna know." He said it like a statement.

"Yeah, I really do," I said. You never get a second chance to make a first impression, I had heard. I knew by now that whatever first impression I made with a new man or a new crew of men, I'd have to live with it. Better the ironworkers see me as no-nonsense and tough right from the get-go. The stakes on my shoulder were heavy and hot, but I stood as solidly as I could, like it was nothing to me to have 30-lbs of hot steel on my shoulder, like I could stand here all day in the blazing California sun, making small talk with some rodbuster.

The man grinned at me, like a grizzly does just before it adds you to its omnivorous diet. "You're just a slippery little cunt, and that's what I'm gonna call you. Little Cunt."

I drew a deep breath and let it out. This shit again, I thought.

All women hate the C-word. For some inexplicable reason, it strikes our ears with more impact than any other horrible thing we've ever been called. Hearing that mean ugly man say it made me what to reach up, grab a steel stake off my shoulder and fling it straight into his leering face. Like in the movies, it would fly swift and true and embed itself point-first into his forehead and he would slowly fall backward, an astonished expression on his face. Serve him right!

Instead, I stood as before, the load digging painfully into my trapezoid muscle, the burn on the side of my neck stinging, the sweat running down my checks, the heat of the day rising in weird waves off the white ground. I held his predatory gaze and slowly nodded my head. I smacked my lips as though tasting something. I tasted salt, the salt of my own labor. It tasted pretty good.

"I like that," I said. "Yeah, it has a pleasant ring to it."

The rodbuster threw his head back and barked a hyena-like laugh. "Great!" he said. "Li'l Cunt it is!" He bent to his task, cutting the bands on bundles of re-bar that had just been unloaded from a big rig. I turned and walked away, feeling dubiously triumphant. You're gonna get called this shit anyway, I told myself, best to act like it's partly your idea. It takes the sting out of it. This was something any pestered school-kid on the playground could tell you. Funny how things never change.

In an hour every ironworker at Corcoran was calling me "Li'l Cunt," but I wasn't the only one given a hateful moniker. They called the male laborers "Butt-boy, spread 'em and weep," the equipment operators were "Fly-shitted Wallpaper, because they mostly hang there on the wall doing nothing and aren't even nice to look at."

Carpenters were "Pansy-handed Pretty Boys who call hot sex jacking off while looking at themselves in the mirror." Cement Finishers were "Poor Suckers who stroked it 'til the cream rose but had to wait four hours for it to get hard and by then it was too late to enjoy it because everybody else had gone home," and masons, in their opinion, were "all wetbacks who had learned their trade making donkey shit into bricks and using cow shit for mortar down in Mexico where a good rain storm would knock your house down around your ears."

Everyone had to suck it up, because not a man (or a woman) was gonna complain about the rodbusters.

The rodbusters all cut off the sleeves of their T-shirts. I guessed this was so they could intimidate the men of the other trades with their bulging muscles, because they certainly had them. It seemed that the left shoulder of all their shirts was worn through to the skin, a large calloused tan deltoid muscle showing through. As I observed them I saw that was because they carry (in tandem, two men to one bundle) bundles of rebar on their left shoulders. Shortly after the rodbusters reported to the job, I started seeing brand new work gloves tossed at random around the job site. Being a thrifty sort (raised that way by my Depression-era mother), I started gathering them up and had about seven stuffed in my lunch box.

One of the ironworkers laughed at me, saying, "What'er ya gonna do with them fuckin' things, Li'l Cunt?"

"Use 'em," I said. "They're brand new."

"Try a pair on," he urged. It was only then I noticed that the gloves were all right-handers. That's when I realized the iron workers only wore one glove, the left one, for carrying and holding rebar, while the ungloved right hand uses the lineman's pliers to twist the wire that binds the pieces of rebar together as they create their grids of re-enforcing steel.

I assisted the platoon of ironworkers as they flexed their bulging muscles, demonstrated their superior wit with snappy patter and cussed their way through several grueling weeks of backbreaking labor building a steel spider web within the formed space. "Bring me some more number nine irons, Cunt. Fuckin' hurry it up, I could jack off three times before you make one fuckin' trip!" It was over 100 degrees and I was running with the steel on my shoulder, but they still cussed and hollered all day long. "I gotta hard-on fer some dobies over here, you slippery cunt, move yer skinny ass and bring 'em before I gotta scamper over there and show ya how it's done and believe me you won't like it the way I do it!"

Carrying dobies (small concrete blocks upon which rebar is laid to create a space between the bar and the ground), rigging bundles of rebar for the crane man to lower into the hole, helping measure and mark out their grids with a large crayon called a keel and laying out the various rebar bends the ironworkers would need as they worked, these are the things I did in the blazing sun under the constant lash of the ironworkers' tongues. Laborers could assist, but only ironworkers could tie-wire the steel together. One thing a union tradesman quickly learns is to always stay within one's work classification. There are certain tools the laborer never touches, like the lineman's pliers of an ironworker or the magnesium float of a cement finisher or the hydraulic controls of heavy equipment.

Being the hardest asses on the job was also on the unwritten job description of the ironworker. No one else tried to compete with them for that chore.

I had just stepped into the plywood porta-john one day and before I could turn and slide the little metal hook into its eye, someone jerked the door open and got inside with me. It was Breezy, the ironworker who first had named me Li'l Cunt.

"Fuck!" I said, my heart racing. He had scared the shit outta me.

"That's just what I'm here fer," Breezy said, showing his broken teeth.

I turned around in the cramped space and faced him. It was hot as a twenty dollar pistol in the tiny shit-house and that was pretty hot because outside it was 102 degrees. The two of us barely fit and the back of my knees were jammed up against the toilet seat.

"Get out of here, Breezy!" I said, glaring up at him.

"Hell, Cunt, what's a little fuck between friends?" He tried to kiss me but I pulled my head back away from his sweaty face.

"We aren't friends," I said.

He grinned. "Well, coworkers, then. Since you went and made this a coed construction job. Least you could do is make it worth my while, havin' a cunt on the job."

He leaned closer, his damp dirty chest pressing against my chin. He stank of sweat, last night's whiskey, diesel fuel, greasy steel, cigarette smoke, cinnamon chewing gum, and that underlying musky male smell. "Won't take long," he added, his hands coming up at me.

I pushed against him. As hard as I could. He took a step back, the door snapping open for a second, letting in the bright light of the outside. I pushed again and one of his feet went out and landed on the dirt. He was halfway out. Maybe Bernie or Clint or Russ or one of the other bosses would come see what was going on, but it was a big job site and the porta-potty was off to one side.

"No, not gonna happen," I said, coming at him, moving towards freedom.

"Why the fuck not, Slippery?" he demanded. "It won't take long and you'll be back to slogging dobies and bar fer me like nothin' happened. You might even fuckin' enjoy it."

"No, I wouldn't and it's not gonna happen," I said clearly, looking right in his face.

"Why the hell not?"

"I only fuck <u>tough</u> men," I lied and pushed past him. "You don't even half qualify," I added. This time he let me go and I heard him give a loud hoot behind me.

Now the problem was, I still had to pee and Breezy was jacking off in the only porta-john on the site.

17

The Family Of Man
In which I find a little kindness among the salt of the earth

"**Mija**," the Mexican man said, "do you wan to come wid us ahfter work and haf *una cervasa*?" We were working side by side stacking concrete blocks on a pallet. The mercury had climbed to 113 degrees for the last two weeks. I had never experienced such heat and sweat was running down my cheeks. *Cervasas frias* sounded mighty good.

"Uh, sure, Rudolfo," I said, "where do you go?"

"We meet at de corner mar-ket, de leetle one wid de mural painted on it. You know de won?" He stacked two blocks, rubbed his dusty calloused hands on his jeans and looked at me. Rudolfo was about sixty, his brown face lined with age and weather. His back was hunched with a lifetime of hard work but his smile was untroubled.

"Sure, I'll stop by there on my way home." My route home led down the main drag of Corcoran and I had seen the little market on the corner, with the mural of the lazy Mexican street with the donkey and the adobe buildings and the *sombrero*ed man dozing in the shade of a palm tree.

"Good, I weel buy you *una cervasa*. Which do you like de best?"

"I love Dos Equis," I said.

"I weel buy you won," Rudolfo said and went to pick up more blocks. I didn't get invited to drink beer with the men after work very often but it did happen once in a while. What I did notice is that I got more invitations from my Mexican coworkers than from my white ones. Perhaps they felt a bond with me because we were both perceived to be second-class citizens on the jobs. Or perhaps, despite their machismo, they got over their prejudices and preconceived notions faster than other men.

When I showed up at the corner market, Rudolfo and the other Mexicans were already on the sidewalk in front, drinking beer. Rudolfo handed me a cold Dos Equis that he had bought for me and we all sat down or stood on the sidewalk, leaning back on the muraled wall. The men spoke in Spanish and I sat companionably sipping my beer. We were all in scuffed boots, soiled jeans and ragged T-shirts, our faces and arms dirty and sweaty with the heat and the day's labor.

Out in front of me across the street lay a railroad switching yard, trains pulled off on spurs lying idle, their great gray flanks spray-painted with a crisscrossing mosaic of gang graffiti. Pickup trucks and beat-up cars drove by and Mexican people strolled past exchanging nods and greetings with the men. A farm labor van pulled up in front of the market and the field workers disembarked, carrying their water jugs and plastic lunch baskets. They were raggeder and dirtier even than were we, and, I knew, got paid a fraction of what we did for work just as hard.

The women farm workers, long cotton scarves wrapped around their heads under ball caps and visors, made their way home along the broken concrete while the men set down their burdens and went inside to buy beer, joining us on the sidewalk.

Soon I was one little white woman in a throng of Hispanic males, all talking in Spanish and laughing, sharing stories about the day's work and tomorrow's promise. Some of the farm workers looked at me curiously, but Rudolfo would say a few words quietly and the men would nod and smile.

This was not where I had come from, these were not the people I had been born among, but in a way they were also my people and this was also my place.   My parents had taught me that I was a member of the Family of Man and in this moment I believed it. I had been invited to share something traditional and timeless.   Though I didn't know what the men were talking about, could only understand one word in twenty, I felt happy to be a part of the conversation. For me it was an affirmation that these men at least held no grudge against me for trying to make a living in the best way I knew how.

It was an acknowledgment that I was a laborer and a worthy one, and that my labor was honored, here among the salt of the earth. I sat in the day's late sun, my butt on the hard sidewalk, back against the painted wall, the beer in my hands, watching the brown-faced men laugh and talk, their heads nodding up and down, their smiles flashing in tired faces.

When my bottle was empty, I left it on the sidewalk, rose to my feet and shook Rudolfo's rough hand.

"*Gracias, Señor*," I said to him.

"*Mañana*," he said, and the other men turned to me and smiled. "*Mañana, mañana,*" we all said and I walked away.

Rudolfo, Juan, Placido and the many other Mexicans I worked with over the years taught me a lot through their quiet example. They did it without the flash and bluster of a go-getter like Dutch but their lesson was as valuable.

They showed me the grace and dignity of the true laborer. These are men who came up from the old country and brought with them their tradition of silent endurance in the face of hardship. They toiled and never complained.   They respected themselves for the inherent value of their work. They understood that nothing gets done without labor and so they honored labor.

I was lucky to have the chance to see them in their threadbare glory. When the going got tough as it often did, I took a leaf from their book. When the work was hard, the hours long, the weather bad and the bosses brutal, I grew a thick skin and endured.

When some men stomped and complained about perceived ill treatment by bosses or companies, I kept my mouth shut and kept my muck-stick moving.

When men beefed that I didn't belong on the job, I let my work speak for me.

18

Vibrator Man
In which I am given a dubious honor

Clint handed me the vibrator and said, "Don't over-vibrate. All the rock'll go to the bottom and all the cream'll rise to the top, but no cold joints either. Don't fail me now, kid."

It was the day of the big cement pour. Several extra laborers from 294 had been sent out to the job, as well as four finishers from the cement mason's union. I gulped at all the responsibility placed on me. If I didn't do this just right, I would screw up the whole job. It was to be a monolithic pour, in other words, the entire oval was to be poured one cement truck after another without stopping and all the cement vibrated together while still wet for no "cold joints" which would weaken the completed structure.

There were to be no fuck-ups or the whole structure would have to be demoed and rebuilt. The place was swarming with inspectors and Bernie looked like he'd have a coronary if there were any fuck-ups. Everyone was on edge and all the FNGs from the hall looked nervous.

Being picked to run the vibrator was a badge of honor among us laborers. But it sure as hell wasn't a gravy job! The vibrator was a heavy instrument about the size of a vacuum cleaner with a long (about 6 foot) stiff hose stinger coming off of it and a steel "donkey dong" at the end. Turning the machine on causes the donkey dong to vibrate. The operator grasps the stinger and pokes the vibrating end into the wet cement. This makes the cement settle into all the cracks and crevasses and fill out the form completely. It also aids in one batch of cement blending and mixing into the next batch, if there is any pause between batches. The failure of two batches to properly blend is what causes cold joints.

I looked at the size of the pour we were about to attempt and realized there was no way I could carry the machine in one hand and handle the stinger at the same time hour after hour. I searched around until I found a canvas safety belt lying about and I slung the heavy vibrator over one shoulder with the belt and a twist of wire. Now all I had to do with my hands was lift and carry the long stinger and drag the hundred feet of extension cord behind me.

The crazy thing was, while I was possibly the single most important person on the monolithic pour besides the "chute-man" (who in this case was actually the hose man, since we were using a cement pumper to place the "mud") I was left to my own devices and no one volunteered to assist me, no one was assigned to be my tender. Turns out I sorely needed a tender.

The extension cord caught on everything, the rebar, the twists of wire holding the rebar together, metal stakes, form wood, nails. I was constantly jerking and pulling and whipping and slinging my extension cord so that I could move freely around the area we were pouring. Because of the importance of my task, I needed that mobility but I fought hard for it, with no one to help me.

To make the job harder for all of us, we were walking on the top tier of three tiers of re-enforcing steel, each tier 10 inches below the previous, in a grid pattern of approximately 12 inches square. As we worked, we had to watch where we placed each step so as not to fall into the space between the bars. We worked with cement-slimed rubber boots on, stepping from bar to bar, trying not to slip off, balancing our weight on the narrow bars of steel under our insteps, trying to perform our job duties, whether handling the hose, shoveling mud or running the vibrator. If you did misstep or your foot slid off a bar, you fell three feet down, your crotch usually hitting the rebar just before your foot hit the ground below. Male or female, slamming your crotch into a number eight rebar with the full force of your body weight behind it is no pleasant experience!

The big cement pumper rig was set up on top, on the edge of the excavation, its long hose dangling out over the job on a system of extending booms. The incoming cement trucks would back up to this rig and empty their load into the hopper of the pumper, one after the other. The pumper would then pump the wet cement up through its hose, out along its booms and down its drop hose into the hands of the chute-man, who pushed and pulled the open end of the drop hose, depositing the mud into the project exactly where he felt it needed to be. The mud streamed and boiled out of the business end of that hose, spraying and splattering in all directions, covering the chute-man, the shovel-men and the vibrator-man with the gray gritty slime.

"Mud" is an appropriate colloquialism for wet cement, for doing a cement pour is much like making mud pies or having a mud wrestling match, except for the fact that while real mud is a benign natural substance, wet cement is actually toxic to humans. More than one man has died of cement poisoning.

You don't want to get it on you! Oh well, on a pour like this, you were gonna get covered. Nothing for it.

In addition to the usual hard hat and gloves, we had to wear safety glasses because the splatter of the mud coated us, including our faces. Getting the stuff in your eye hurts like hell and can damage your vision. The goggles and safety glasses handed out by the foreman seemed to distort my depth perception, which had made it hard for me not to misstep and fall through the rebar grid while working on this job.

Several weeks of barking my shins and smashing my crotch against rebar had sent me to an eye doctor for an exam. My vision was 20/20 as it had always been. How then, I asked the doctor, could I get a pair of safety glasses which did not distort my depth perception? He built me a pair of tinted safety glasses with UV protection and added the slightest prescription to them so that my health insurance provided by the union would pay for most of it. I paid 70 bucks out of pocket and the policy paid $200. Even so it was the most I would ever spend on glasses or sunglasses in my life and I had been hard pressed to afford it.

These prized glasses were on my face when the monolithic pour began.

19

The Monolithic Pour
In which I struggle against an old man's pride and a really big vibrator

My friend Juan was chute-man.
He smiled at me. *"Listo,* Eh-mee?"

"Sî, Señor, listo," I said, gripping my stinger, ready to plunge it into the mud. He signaled to the pumper operator and the fun began. The 6-inch hose between Juan's gnarled hands jerked and twitched and within a few minutes the gray-green cement began to pour from it, flumping and splooshing onto the rebar, flowing down through the grid, spreading across the gravel bed, covering the first tier of re-enforcing steel.

Juan gave me the nod and I reached back and switched on the vibrator. The thing slung at my side thrummed loudly into life and the stiff stinger in my gloved hands vibrated, jangling my very phalanges. I leaned forward and stuck the steel donkey dong between the rebar into the cement. The vibration liquefied the mud where it had heaped up and caused it to continue to flow.

I had to be careful only to move the mud into any hollow spaces and make sure it filled out the form completely. If I saw the sheen across the surface or a bubble of air forming, I was over-vibrating. I would quickly jerk the stinger back out of the mud. Sometimes the donkey dong would get wedged between the rebar grids below the mud and I couldn't pull it out quickly. Juan would turn and glare at me, knowing that I might be over-vibrating. He could not necessarily know the thing was stuck, being actively caught up in moving the hose around and signaling the pumper operator. If the donkey dong got stuck in the rebar, I would have to switch the machine off and tug and pull until I got it free. Then I would be behind, Juan would have filled another area and I would have to scramble to get caught up. I would earn another glare from the old man.

Meanwhile, several shovel men were up to their boot tops in the mud, pushing it this way and that with their muck-sticks, mostly getting in my way. The FNGs from the hall were all trying to show that they were hard workers, and throughout the day at different times we would have use for all of them, but there were also times when too many chefs spoil the broth. I could have used one to be my tender, but I could not tell any of them what to do. Bernie the Super and Clint the foreman were up on top near the pumper watching the activity with bated breath, so I could not ask them to assign me a tender. I just had to do my best.

The shovel jockeys were all in the way, pushing mud around, keeping me from doing what I needed to do. The vibrator moves mud too and if the shovel men had stepped back once in a while to let me in, they could have saved themselves some sweat, but they were nervous newbies and wouldn't lean on their muck-sticks for an instant! In fact, a couple of them squawked at me when I pulled the donkey dong out and it sprayed mud on them before I stuck it back in. As if they and I and Juan weren't already covered with the stuff!

So to please them I tried shutting it off when I pulled it out and turning it on when I shoved it back in. Click. Click. Click. Click. Click. Click.

Juan saw me do this and hollered over the noise. "Eh-mee, hef you never been vibrator man? Never turn it off, just kep it going! Kep it going!" Feeling chastised, I determined never to shut it off unless it was wedged in the rebar, the FNGs would just have to bitch! The noise from the vibrator was deafening in my ear, making it hard to hear Juan's instructions. I had to watch my vibration but also keep one eye on the old man to make sure he wasn't talking to me. When the shovel men got in the way, I was looking to see how I could maneuver myself and my tool around them as well. Juan threw his ancient shoulder against the hose, pushing the business end of it this way and that, mud flying here and then there.

"Eh-mee!" he hollered and when I looked up, his finger was pointing to a spot I had missed in the confusion. I couldn't get myself and the vibrator with its trailing cord to him quickly enough. "Here, here, here!" he hollered, snapping his fingers and gesturing, as the mud continued to pour nonstop. I elbowed my way in, sticking my vibrator where I needed it to be, even causing one or two of the shovel men to lose their balance and fall through the grid. Now the shovel men glowered and swore at me. Not making any friends, I thought. Shit!

As we worked our way back and forth across the oval, the distance grew wider and wider. The shovel men could just follow Juan and the hose but I had the vibrator, stinger and the extension cord to move, and the cord catching on everything! As the cord lay across the rebar, a loop of it would fall down into the grid and when I went to pull up the slack, the loop would hook on something down below. Jerking and pulling on the cord would not free it. The only way was to go over there and bend down, reach in and unhook it. If I unslung the harness from over my head and set down the vibrator, went back and did this, Juan would yell at me because I wasn't vibrating the cement as it was being placed. If I left the vibrator on and tried to run back, bend over, reach in and unhook the cord, more cord that I was dragging behind me would hook on something else.

It was a terrible Catch-22 and as I struggled, I kept thinking that one of those guys would put down his muck-stick and come help me, or that Juan, being the Venerable Laborer of the crew, would say to someone, "You put down your *pala*, go help Eh-mee. What she needs, do it for her. We need her to be at the hose *listo* all the time."

All I got was those faces turned towards me expectantly, like, why are you dilly-dallying? So, I strained and struggled and tried to be where the mud was. After the first few hours of this, my shoulders ached, the nerves in my hands were jangling, my legs were exhausted, my back was in spasm and the bottoms of my feet were bruised from the rebar. As I stepped painfully from bar to bar, trying to balance the heavy vibrator and my own weight as I tugged and pulled on my leash of an extension cord, I promised my feet that if such an animal existed as rubber boots with steel shanks, I would buy a pair!

My clothes were covered with a layer of cement both wet and dried, and the layer of dried cement on my face felt like heavy stage makeup that cracked when I grimaced, which was often. My safety glasses had been covered with cement splatters so thoroughly that I had had to clean them three times in order to see out of them, but now the bandana in my pocket was so filthy it no longer could do the job. I ruefully recalled Dr. Narahara instructing me on the careful cleaning of the glasses to enhance their life span. "Use a soft chamois and contact lens solution, buff them softly, being careful not to grind any particles into the safety glass." If he could see me and my glasses now!

The trucks roared in, streaming white dust and diesel fumes, unloading their messy loads into the hopper, the pumper kept pumping, the mud kept coming down the hose, splattering everywhere, the shovel men kept getting in my way and Juan kept glaring and hollering at me. The cement finishers from the mason's union were working along behind us, floating and finishing the cement. The sun beat down and the temperature in the hole was in the nineties. There were no breaks, not even for lunch because the nature of a monolithic pour is that it stops for nothing!

The shovel jockeys and Juan periodically got to run to the side and drink water from a jug while they waited for the next truck to line up and back in, but I was always using any short break in the frenetic activity to untangle my cord and haul my vibrator to the area below the hose. My mouth and throat were parched, and I had sweat every drop of moisture out of me. Heat waves seemed to float before my eyes.

Hour after hour passed and I worked in a state of resignation, enduring the pains of my body, the effects of heat and thirst and the frustration that no one would help me. The vibrator weighed heavy on my shoulder strap and, vibrating hot against my hip bone, slowly built a blue bruise that would not go away for three weeks. It was late in the afternoon and the monolithic pour was about ¾ completed, when I finally yelled at the old man.

Juan had signaled the pumper operator to swing the boom from one side of the pour to the other in order to maneuver around an interior wall configuration. The whole crew began to move, shovels in hand, leaving me behind to deal with my equipment. As I made to follow, my cord snagged on the rebar behind me, the stinger slipped from my wet cement-saturated glove and the donkey dong fell between two tiers of rebar matting in front of me, wedging firmly. I could hear the sound of the mud flooshing and splumping into the pour, heard the men driving their shovels into the cement, heard Juan bark for vibration. "Eh-mee! Vibrate!"

I stopped, poised on my aching insteps on two bars, pulled with one hand at the bound cord and with the other at the stuck donkey dong, neither of which gave in the slightest. I glanced over to see Juan's face and the expectant faces of the newbies. They stared back at me as the mud come down. Harder, I tugged again at the cord and again at the stinger, then one foot slid off a bar and down I went into the steel spider web! My knee struck the second tier rebar, ripping my jeans and my skin, my kneecap slamming hard against the ridged surface of the re-enforcing steel.

I pitched forward, letting loose my grip on the stinger and throwing both my hands out. One hand grabbed rebar, somewhat bracing my fall, the other missed and drove down into the second tier, ripping my skin on sharp tie-wire as it went and my wrist jammed painfully against rebar, spraining it. Bright white-hot lights went through my head at the sudden pain! Meanwhile, the three foot drop had slammed my pubis into rebar with a bone-numbing impact and nerve explosions raced through me to my very finger tips, nearly causing a blackout.

When my foot finally hit bottom, fractions of a second too late for my poor pubis, my ankle sprained. As to my other leg, the knee came down hard on the top tier of rebar, slamming bone against steel. The heavy vibrator still strapped to my body, ended up wedged between my already sore hipbone and the rebar, digging into my ribs and scoring the skin off of my right side. As if this wasn't bad enough, my $70 safety glasses were pitched from my face and I heard them land with a crash and a tinkle about 15 feet away! God-damned mother-fucking son of a bitch! My god-damned mother-fucking glasses!

Like a dragonfly squashed in the grill of a passing big rig, I was firmly imbedded in the rebar, unable to move, body parts wedged in between bars, clothing and skin hooked on sharp wire, tangled in extension cord, wrapped in stinger hose and harness belt and immobilized by sundry pains, both dully aching and stingingly sharp. My head swam with heat and dehydration and the hundred little agonies of scraps, cuts, bone contusions and bruises. As I lay there, pinned like a bug on the collector's table, catching my breath and assessing my damages, I had a sudden thought that at least I had not bit my tongue as I landed. Small blessing! I almost laughed.

I wiggled, testingly, trying to see in what way I could begin to extricate myself. I fully expected that at any moment someone, or perhaps two people, would appear to help me get up, but I wanted to have started getting up by the time they got here, so that they wouldn't just grab and start to jerk, ripping my skin further on the wire and bar and things they couldn't see. As I began to move and free parts of me and my equipment, some sounds began to intrude upon my awareness. Yelling. Hollering. I glanced over at where the men were. The mud was streaming down from the hose, shovel men were pushing mud around, Juan was holding the hose end and his red infuriated face was looking towards me and his voice was heard over the din.

"Eh-mee! What you doing?! *Andale*, get over here. Vibrate! Vibrate!"

No one was coming to help me. I pushed the harness off over my head, unwedged the vibrator from between me and the rebar and shoved it aside. I pulled my sprained wrist from between two pieces of re-enforcing steel and used that hand to grasp a bar, wincing with the pain as I pushed myself up. My pants were caught on wire down below and as I pulled my leg out, my skin ripped some more. I dragged myself to my feet, balancing dizzily on two bars, squared my hard hat back on my head, rubbed my skinned and bruised elbows and knees briefly with my hands, and went back to unhook the extension cord and pull enough slack free to get me where the crew was.

Juan's voice. "Eh-mee, hurry up! Vibrate! Vibrate! What you doing!?"

My self-imposed rule of no complaining was beginning to seem like too great a burden. As I ran wobbling back to the vibrator, moving fast but trying not to fall through again, I hollered back, "I am going as fast as I can, Juan! I could use a little help!" This last was rhetorical, as I figured if no one had helped me yet, no one really would help me now. I was right, no one did. "Hurry up!" was all the response I got, "Hurry up! what you doing!?"

I bent over, grabbed the strap of the harness and slung it over my head, jerking and pulling on the stinger, trying to free it from its lodging in the rebar matting. Both forearms were bleeding from a dozen abrasions and my left elbow didn't want to bend anymore. My right glove had been lost in the fall and the hand bled profusely from several bad wire cuts, red blood mixing with the gray cement slime on the stinger of the vibrator. Cement and sweat made the cuts sting fiercely. I had to pull hard several times to get the donkey dong free.

"What you doing?!"

"Juan!" I yelled back, "Stop acting like an asshole! Get someone to help me!"

The donkey dong unwedged and flew back towards me, almost toppling me backwards. I caught my balance and began running as fast as I could to the crew, carrying my unwieldy load and dragging my long leash behind me. I switched on the machine as I approached and thrust the thing into the heaps of mud which had accumulated at Juan's feet. I glanced at the old man's face. It was stone.

I had worked with the old guy on the Sierra Project and on many other jobs. I had visited with him between jobs at the union hall, where the old laborers played cards and dominos in the loft most weekends. He had always taught me how things were done and been kind to me, and I had always treated him with respect, addressing him as "Señor." We had always liked each other.

The look on the Venerable's face now was terrible to behold. His black eyes burned in their sockets unblinkingly for a moment, his brown cheeks were hard and unyielding, no reminder of the smiles which had made them mobile. His teeth with their old gold caps were hidden from me now, those teeth often bared in a sassy grin. He looked at me a moment, sullen and stern and then slowly he turned his face away. The old man never looked my way again, not once in the next nine years I would know him. Juan was done with me.

The monolithic pour was completed, without a hitch, at least from the lofty point of view of Bernie and the company. No rock pockets, no soft spots, no cold joints. The crew had worked nonstop from 7 a.m to 9 p.m and the trucks had come in one after the other without a break. The pumper had operated flawlessly and the inspectors were satisfied. The sewer plant project would continue.

Besides a few minor injuries (most of them on me) no one had been hurt. In fact there were only two causalities of note. My broken safety glasses and my friendship with the old man. Years later, working on a job with Juan's son John, who followed in his father's footsteps and became a member of Laborer's 294, John told me that I had deeply hurt his old man that day by calling him an asshole.

"My father was never disrespected as you disrespected him that day." Shit, I thought, the old man ought to try being me, I don't get all bent outta shape by being disrespected. I just live with it.

I explained to the son, first the situation that had driven me to that extremis and secondly that I did not call Juan an asshole only that I implored him not to act like an asshole. This subtly was lost upon the son, as it had been upon the father.

"You called my father an asshole and he never forgave you for that. He says he never spoke with you again."

"No, he never did."

"Even though you worked together on several more jobs."

"Yes, even though we did."

The monolithic pour and the old man's pride seemed to me the same. Hard, immovable, unstoppable, subject neither to present circumstance nor past history. The pour could not be paused, not for any reason. The old man could not be disrespected, not for any reason. No room for flexibility, either in the pour or the pride. Stories of men buried in Hoover dam came to mind, they too were victims of the monolithic pour and they lost their lives. All I lost was skin, a friend, and pair of glasses.

"You could always try apologizing to him," the son suggested.

I thought back to my days in the National Park Service, where the battle between men and women in the workplace was largely over, with the exception of a few small skirmishes. Having left that neutral ground and traveled into No Woman's Land, I had to face my Minotaurs. Backing down would not serve me.

I could sweat and slave and get down and dirty with the people of the body and I could keep pace elbow to elbow with the best of 'em. I could take a lot of shit, put up with a lot of crap, but I wasn't going to lick any boots and I damn-sure wasn't gonna grovel!

"No," I said, thinking but not saying that the old man owed me an apology, if anything. All these assholes did. "No, I can't do that."

I had to work with these men. In so many ways I had to become like them.

20

No Ugly Women
In which my face is slightly rearranged

"Hey, Emmy, I forget *mi pala!*" Rudolfo yelled. "Toss won hop to me!"

We had formed up a section of 12-inch-thick wall to be poured. The steel-ply forms had scaffolding for workers along the top about twenty feet above the monolithic slab. We had formed a section about forty feet long and twenty feet high and the first cement trucks were arriving. I was on the bottom rung of a ladder, climbing up to the work platform on the scaffold when Rudolfo asked for a shovel. I had a length of extension cord for the vibrator in my hand, otherwise I would have carried the shovel up the ladder with me, but I decided to do like he had said and toss the damn thing. I got off the ladder, put down my cord and picked up the shovel. Rudolfo leaned out over the railing of the scaffold above me and held out a hand.

"*Andale!*" he shouted.

I grabbed the butt-end of the shovel handle in one hand and the shaft below the head in the other, gave one of those old one, two, three deals and chucked that shovel straight up as hard as I could. It flew straight up and was looking good until the blade of the shovel caught the underside edge of a scaffold bracket Clang! and it suddenly reversed course.

The butt of the shovel came down into my mouth. Whacko!

It put me flat on my back. When I rolled over onto my knees, I was spitting blood and pieces of tooth out onto the slab. Both my lips were split wide open and a front tooth was shattered. I staggered up and ran my hand over my mouth, wiping away blood. Rudolfo shouted, "Oh, sheet! Emmy, you ahl right?"

"Yez," I said. I was a little dizzy but okay. I waited a moment for the dizziness to pass then bent and picked up the shovel, grabbed up my roll of cord and began to climb the ladder. No time to worry about my tooth right now. We had a cement pour to do!

Before I had gone five feet up the ladder, someone grabbed me by the belt loops and jerked me back to the ground. "Lemme see that puss," the carpenter foreman Clint growled. I turned towards the gruff old guy. He tsk-tsked over my bleeding lips which I had pressed together, hiding my teeth. "Very nice," he snarled. "Like you been in a bar fight. Now open up!"

I parted my lips and he peered in. "Just as I thought! Sorry, kid, you're outta here!"

"But we gozza zement pour!" My words whistled strangely through the gap in my teeth.

Clint said, "Look, I barely allow women on my jobs, and sure as loose shit in a stiff wind ain't gonna allow no ugly women on my jobs! It'll make me look bad and what's worse, it'd made the comp'ny look bad. So, skidaddle off to a dentist and I don't wanna see this ugly puss of yours again, you hear me?"

I stood there stupidly. Was I being fired?

"Go on, get yer skinny little ass outta here. Don't come back 'til yer pretty again! Don't worry, I'll have somebody else vibrate this one. They might not do as nice a job as you, but we'll live with it."

"Oh, okay, bozz," I said.

"Now git!" Clint barked, "and when you come back bring the dentist bill with you!" I turned to go and Clint hollered after me, "And kid, no more shovel-chuckin' for you! You ain't that good at it!"

I was back the next day, and Clint pried open my mouth to inspect Dr. Silverman's work. I liked Clint, he was an old cattle-roper and had lost the first two joints of his right index and middle fingers in a roping accident. I can't count how many Estwing hammers of mine he lost inside the concrete walls of that sewer plant by borrowing them ("hey, kid, hand me your hammer for a second!") and then losing his grip on them as he tried to correct some problem in the forms. Ping ping ping! they'd go down inside the steel-ply through the re-bar. Those hammers are now part of the re-enforcing steel in the concrete. Clint would always buy me a nice new hammer. I still have the last one he bought me.

"Not bad for a rush job!" the foreman said, looking at my teeth.

"I'm starting to feel like a horse," I said.

"Well, kid, it's better than lookin' like this," Clint grinned broadly at me and revealed a mouth with six front teeth missing.

"Fightin'," he said before I could ask. "As painful as getting clobbered in the mouth with a shovel, but a helluvalot more fun! And if you think this is bad, you shoulda seen the other guy!"

"Yeah, but boss..." I said.

"What?"

"On you, it's a good look."

Clint smiled. "Thanks, kid. Now get to work, before I tramp you outta here for real."

Amy R Farrell

21

A Dangerous Operator
In which I damn near get killed

Randy was kind of an old school dinosaur who would either die or retire before he'd ever accept women on the job. He was a heavy equipment operator and damned good one, the kind of guy who could jump on any machine, large or small, and operate it like it was an extension of his body. Such workers are worth their weight in gold, not to mention they are a joy to watch.

One man I knew, Trent, who was one of these "golden" operators, could pick up a coin off the ground and deposit it into your pocket, using a Komatsu excavator with a three-foot-wide thumbed bucket. Granted, you had to hold the pocket open for him and you ended up with dirt in your pocket as well as a quarter, but hey! This guy Randy was that good, but unlike Trent, I wouldn't trust him to get that near me.

Randy's favorite trick to get my goat was using his crane to dangle heavy loads over my head while I was working. I first worked with him when I was assigned by Clint to be his load-slinger. I would chain up bundles of rebar, bundles of lumber, or generators, compactors or other heavy tools to be lowered by crane down into the pit. Randy would sit there in his air-conditioned cab, hands on his controls, grinning at me like some kind of demented Cheshire cat.

I would be working in the San Joaquin Valley heat, sweating bullets in dry 100 degree air, sunshine beating down on me as I crawled around in the white alkali dust, running a chain under a bundle of something. He would honk his horn impatiently as I struggled to throw a half-hitch with the chain, and he would lower the heavy iron hook on its long rusty cable until it bumped me on my hard hat. I would bat it away, or move out from under it and scowl at Randy. He would grin and work his controls just so the hook would start a slow and gentle swinging back and forth. He'd swing it and lower it just so it would bump me on the helmet when I wasn't looking. A couple times he knocked my hard hat off my head with his damned hook! The hook game escalated until after a while he would lower huge objects over me, no matter what I was doing, no matter what he was supposed to be doing.

I might be minding my own business, helping the carpenters build forms and all of a sudden I would get that feeling that someone was watching me. Glancing around, I'd catch Randy's eye, see his nasty grin, and look up to see a generator hanging over my head. He might be in his crane a half a job away but the reach of the crane was so great, he could hang things over my head without me even knowing, pretty much no matter where I was on the job site. It became his little game, waiting to see how long it would take me to notice.

Having things that could crush the life out of me hanging over my head wasn't something I approved of. I didn't much like the look of the rusty cable on the crane. Who knew the last time the thing had been inspected, weight-tested or replaced? I thought Randy was taking an awful risk, trusting that a freak accident didn't occur and take my life and possibly cost him his license. Even if he cared nothing for me, his job would be at stake.

Later, when we started forming and pouring the wall sections of the sewer plant, Randy's crane would lower the cement to us in three-yard buckets suspended from the cable. The cement trucks would dispense the mud into the bucket which then would be hooked to the cable and the crane would fly it over to where we laborers stood on the scaffold platform twenty feet above the concrete slab. Two laborers would grab the huge metal bucket as Randy swung it over, slow its swing to a standstill over the top of the form, and with a jerk on the handle, dump the wet cement into the form, where it would plummet all the way to the bottom, twenty feet below.

I would switch on the vibrator and lower a special super-long stinger down into the forms, while the guys waited for Randy to get another bucket load. Sometimes, Randy would get the loaded bucket before we were quite ready for it, and he would hold it in the air waiting for us. On those occasions, he liked to position the bucket over my head. I would be vibrating or performing some other task and I'd feel a drop of something wet and cold hit the back of my neck. I'd look up and sure enough, there'd be the bucket of cement suspended about ten feet above me. If the cable or hook failed, or if the ring on the top of the bucket broke, I would be dead. This behavior went on for months.

I was determined not to complain to the bosses, because I felt that a complaint against another worker would land me on some kind of blacklist. Especially against a respected and valued worker like Randy. I was only hired off the board. I could be replaced. A reputation as a girl who couldn't handle the stress of the job was not something I wanted and I knew that's what I'd get if I complained about anything. Anything at all. Just do the work, I told myself.

So I kept a stiff upper lip and just did the work. I also believed that "the truth will out." I hoped that Clint or even Bernie the job super would notice the recklessness of the crane operator and put an end to it before something bad happened. But as it turned out, it took me almost getting killed before anyone noticed.

One day, during the pour, we had a minor blow-out of the form and stopped to make repairs. The other laborers and I were on hands and knees up on the scaffold, pounding with hammers trying to get the form braced. Randy had a full bucket of mud hanging there waiting for us. He had it about three feet over my head and was playing with his controls, getting the bucket to swing lazily back and forth. I felt a drop of cold cement slop hit my neck and glanced up. My coworker, a guy named Miguel, who was on his knees working right next to me, looked up also and saw the swinging bucket. He glared over at the crane operator, gesturing for him to move the bucket away, and Randy grinned at us. Randy hated Mexicans as much as he hated women.

We were so absorbed in fixing the form, aware that the whole day's work was waiting on us that we forgot about Randy and the swinging bucket. "Okay, I think that's got it," Miguel said and he and I stood up. The bucket slammed into me, knocking me backwards. I felt the 2x4 rails of the scaffolding strike my back as I was pinned between them and the bucket. The wind was knocked out of me and I heard a loud crack as the top rail broke. The bucket was still swinging, pushing me back over the void. I threw my hands up, grasping the sloppy lip of the mud bucket. The cold metal was slippery and gritty with wet cement, but I held on to it. The railing broke free from the bracket and I heard the wood land with a slap on the concrete floor twenty feet below me.

My feet left the scaffold, dangling out over nothing. Looking over my shoulder, I saw emptiness. The bucket still pushed, not yet having reached the apex of its swing. I held onto the lip, knowing that as long as I didn't let go, the bucket would change direction and carry me back onto the safety of the platform again. The time seemed interminable, however.

My fingers began to slip.

I was still hanging out over empty space.

Then I saw Miguel. He too had been bumped by the bucket as he stood, but it had dealt him only a glancing blow whereas it had struck me full-on. Now he reached out and grabbed the other side of the swinging bucket and threw his weight backwards, helping to speed the return of the pendulum. As it slowed, paused for an endless second, then began to swing back, I watched for the moment when my feet were back over wood and I could put them down on the planking. At that moment, my fingers slipped off the bucket. But the planks were below me and I landed on my feet back on the platform, my heart pounding. I stepped away from the bucket, and Miguel let go of it.

Miguel rounded on Randy, red fury in his cheeks. He let fly a string of expletives in Spanish. At least that is what they must have been, because they were said with great passion and I don't think they were proclamations of undying love. Miguel expressed what I was feeling. I was too shaken up by the brush with death to do anything but stand there and wait until I stopped shaking.

After a minute, I gave Randy a cold stare and started working.

I think the shit hit the fan after that, because it was the last time Randy played his game. That operator had almost killed me.

The statistics on construction accidents show that 90% of falls from a height of eleven feet or over result in death, so a fall from the height of that scaffold onto solid concrete would have been the end of me.

It was only luck that the bucket hit me in the chest so that I could grab on with my hands and that, despite the slippery edge, I was able to hold on long enough, and that Miguel was there to help pull the bucket back.

Otherwise you wouldn't be reading this book.

22

Side Job

In which I damned near get killed

Angelina's was the kind of small-town cafe where the waitresses all knew you and the names of the regulars were painted on the backs of the chairs they always sat in. Neil, the local tree-trimmer, was one of the locals with whom I'd pick up work in the off-season or on weekends for some extra cash. He would hold court in the "Neil" chair and buy his workers breakfast (scrambled eggs, hash browns and toast for me) and we'd get stoked on good fresh hot coffee before jumping in his beat-up old truck to go to work. Lunchtime, we'd head back to the cafe for lunch, also on Neil's tab.

"If I'm gonna work you half to death, least I can do is feed you," Neil said that Saturday as we met for breakfast. I would've jumped over the moon for the guy! The way to this little construction worker's heart is definitely through her stomach.

We left Angelina's after stuffing our faces and drove down to Lemon Cove, a nearby town, where there was a grand old three-story home with a massive eucalyptus tree in the yard. The owner was worried that this huge tree would someday topple onto the house or at least drop a big limb on it. Neil's job for the day was to "top" the tree. The word doesn't do justice to the magnitude of the project. By the time it was done, Neil had cut half of that tree out and it was still a very big tree! When we pulled into the yard to start the job, I looked in amazement at the size of it. It was one of the biggest Eucs I had ever seen and I had grown up on the California coast, where monster eucalyptus trees grow all over the place.

The tree was about 150 feet high, with a bole that wouldn't have shamed a giant Sequoia. About twelve feet up the tree split into three separate trunks, each of them three feet in diameter. At the apex of these three trunks was a big tangle of sticks and bark which proved to be the nest of a Great Horned Owl, who glared and hooted at us the entire time we worked on the tree, but who refused to leave her clutch of eggs.

Neil belted on his harness and hung his small chainsaw from his belt. He never wore climbing spurs because he didn't believe in harming the tree with hooks. He climbed the tree, nimbly with his lengths of bull rope over his shoulder. He performed his aerial act there above me, setting up his safety lines. I felt sick just watching him up there but he seemed as at home as a koala in that big gum tree. He was so far up that I got a crick in my neck trying to keep an eye on him as he climbed.

Once I got the big old brush chipper running (it was so ancient that getting it to start in the morning usually required several offerings to the patron saints of tree-trimmers, not to mention an aerosol can of ether and some really bad cuss words), I then proceeded to lay out the loppers and the chain saws I would be using and waited for the brush to start falling from the sky.

Somewhere up above, out of sight in the swaying graceful limbs of the venerable old tree, I heard Neil's saw start. It was a small chain saw that he kept tethered to his safety harness on a short rope so he could drop it anytime he wanted and it wouldn't fall all the way down, just far enough away to be out of his way but within his reach when he needed to pull it back up hand over hand. He had the throttle set so that the minute his finger left the trigger, the engine would die. This meant he had to pull the cord to restart it every time but it was safer for him in case something went very wrong up there. When he moved about in the tree from place to place and restrung his ropes from one area of the tree to another, the little saw bobbed along below him on its leash.

I stood back out of the way until the first limbs started falling, so that I could pinpoint where Neil was beginning. They came crashing down, hitting the ground in a cloud of dust, leaves and eucalyptus nuts. Each limb was about twenty feet long, laden with offshoot branches, ribbon-like peeling bark and long curved scented leaves. I'd rush in, grab a limb and drag it towards the chipper where I would buck it up into pieces, cut the firewood out of it and run all the smaller stuff through the chipper. Then I'd rush in and grab another limb. I had to keep looking up to make sure I didn't get underneath Neil when he was dropping something, and he would try to keep an eye on me to make sure I wasn't under him when he did.

At some point in the proceedings, Neil would have to take out large hunks of tree trunk and I would simply get out of the way and watch the huge pieces fall. Chunks six feet long and two feet in diameter would drop as if in slow motion, tumbling end over end and Kathunk! hit the ground in a cloud of dust. When it was all clear, Neil would take a high altitude break and I would grab the big chain saw and buck the logs into 24 inch rounds and roll them off to stack near the house for later splitting.

The way Neil sharpened his saws was a thing of beauty, long white curls of pungent wood chips would fly from under the rotating chain, piling at my feet. Cutting through that wet eucalyptus wood was like cutting through butter with a hot knife!

Once I had the big rounds cleared away under one part of the tree, Neil would realign his ropes and swing over to another part of the tree, allowing me to work on the existing brush heap while he dropped limbs elsewhere.

Usually this system worked well. On this one day, however, Neil moved to the other side of the big eucalyptus and I got busy cleaning up after him on the opposite side. Perhaps we both got a little too comfortable and stopped paying attention to where the other person was. All I know is I heard a crack directly above me and when I looked up, part of the tree was coming down on top of me. I didn't even have time to jump, a huge limb thudded into the ground, the heavy end sinking into the soft earth a mere 12 inches from my right foot.

The limb was twenty-five feet long and its cut end (the end that landed near me) was 10 inches in diameter. If it had struck me, it would have killed me, no doubt about it. I looked at the limb, then craned my neck and looked up. Neil was a hundred feet directly above me, looking down. His face was ashen and his eyes as big as saucers.

The little chain saw swung on its tether from his belt, back and forth like a pendulum, ticking out the seconds of our lives. I smiled and shrugged my shoulders. Neil smiled and shook his head. Then we both laughed. What else was there to do? It was a momentary lapse of attention that could have cost me my life and changed Neil's forever. But it was over. And there was work to do.

Always more work to do. Each time something potentially deadly happened on a job whoever was involved simply laughed, shrugged, and went back to work. Because the work didn't get done by dreaming about it. And it would never get done if people were too scared to do it!

Even if someone did die, the rest went back to work, like the day the previous week on the prison job. It happened over at the Smith and Walerman site, where some guys I knew from the hall were working. I saw the emergency vehicles arrive and word flew around that a man had died. After work Rudolfo and the other Mexicans and I went over to the scene to take a look. Rudolfo said a prayer in Spanish while we all bowed our heads.

It was a simple mistake that cost the man his life.

A tilt-up was being raised into position by a crane operator who was clear on the other side, unable to see the crew for whom he was moving material. Radio communications informed the operator what to do. The tilt-up was a section of concrete wall about eight-inches thick and perhaps twenty feet wide by twenty-five feet high. The cell blocks of the prison were all constructed by the tilt-up method, that is, sections of wall were poured in forms on the ground, then lifted into position by cranes and fastened together by workers. Huge metal braces would be attached to hold the section in place until it could be permanently fastened into the existing wall. The crane operator would hold the piece steady until given the order via the radio to release it.

As I heard the story, at that week's safety meeting the company bosses had harangued the crew that they needed to step up the pace if the company was to make deadline. They needed more tilt-ups placed per day than they were currently getting, or heads were gonna roll. Everybody being job-scared, they put on the hustle. The man who was squashed by the tilt-up was the radio man who directed the crane operator. He issued the release order prematurely, thinking that the guys had finished bracing the section.

The tilt-up came down and he was under it.

Cal-Osha closed that part of the job site down and work there didn't resume for a week or more. So the company didn't make deadline anyway! When we snuck under the incident tape after work to sneak a peek, we could see where the tilt-up had been lifted to remove the body. There was nothing there but fluids soaked into the ground.

It was a wake-up call for everyone on the project. No matter what anyone says, never sacrifice safety for production. Of course, in reality, that was easier said than done, for in my experience, bosses were always cutting corners and driving the workers hard. No one wants to lose a good-paying job or be blacklisted by a pissed-off job super.

But no one wants to die either.

23

Rough Accommodations
In which I sleep surrounded by the barbarian horde

Carefully loading each chamber of the old Colt .38, I spun the cylinder with a well-oiled Whirr! and snapped the cylinder back into the gun's frame. Sliding the weapon under my pillow, I lay back in my sleeping bag and stared at the ribbed metal ceiling of my camper-shell. It was almost dark and so cold my breath froze in the air as I exhaled. I shivered with cold and with fear. Outside the wind whipped through the pines and stirred up the sandy soil of the lake bottom, gusting it against the battered paint of my Toyota, rocking the old truck on its springs.

It had been so windy that I had had to heat my can of vegetarian chile on my Svea backpacking stove inside my camper-shell rather than on the tailgate, trying not to set the bedding on fire. I had peeled the paper label off and heated the can right on the little blue flame and eaten the spicy chili straight out of the can. No dishes to wash. This was a simple bivouac after all, not a real camp. I wasn't even supposed to be here and I hoped the rangers wouldn't monkey-shine me in the middle of the night.

I was a stranger in a strange land.

The company I had worked for most of that summer had invited me to join one of their crews on a job at Shaver Lake, quite a distance from my home in Three Rivers. The job was winding down but before the snow flew they wanted to see how much more they could get done, and I had proved to be pretty kick-ass on the other job.

No matter how kick-ass, however, if I arrived late for my first day on the new job, the foreman would send me home. Never having been to Shaver Lake, I hadn't known how long it would take me to get there, so instead of leaving early on Monday morning, I had chosen to leave Sunday afternoon and spend the night on the job site. I had found the place just before dark, Edison Campground, closed-for-renovation, on the banks of the lake. Late in the year, the water level was low, exposing vast silty, sandy, and muddy expanses dropping gradually towards the steel-gray waters. Here and there around the lake, I could see bonfires burning, the flames blowing sideways with great devils of sparks swirling off of them, and hear the voices of men, drunk and rowdy, as they partied with their four-wheelers pulled up to the water's edge.

It was deer season and the hunters were out in force. It was a men's game, there probably wasn't another woman on this lake and I sure as hell didn't want them to know I was here. They were wound up pretty tight and they had guns. I had a gun too, but I sure wasn't looking for trouble. If I could get through this night undiscovered in my flimsy camper-shell, tomorrow would be a new day. If not, who knew what tomorrow would bring.

I heard gunshots and lifted my head to peer out. Five hundred feet away, figures danced and cavorted around a fire. The shadowed forms held long-necked beer bottles and I heard glass breaking against stone. Laughter. There was the splash of a beer bottle in the water. One figure had a rifle in hand, and I heard the sound of a bolt ratcheting back and a shell being chambered. Then a shot. More laughter.

"What the hell am I doing here?" I said to myself and was startled to hear the quaver in my voice. "Keep your head down," I said, laying it back on the pillow. "Hopefully those jerks won't shoot at the truck."

Lying there in the cold, the hard truck-bed under my back barely padded by my backpacking Insolite pad, I listened to the buffeting of the wind and the noise of the barbarian hordes and prayed for dawn. In the light of day, the faces of the wildmen would metamorphose into the visages of civilized people. I was born to the people of the mind but I had made my way among the people of the body. These wildmen, I was sure, were people of the body and in the light they would recognize me as one of them, an adopted member of their tribe, and worthy of respect. Tonight, however, I would probably be fair game.

I fell into a fitful slumber. Long twisting, turning, shivering hours later, I started awake. The wind had died and I could clearly hear that which had wakened me. The crunch of footfalls. Voices, close. Soft laughter.

I lay still, the only part of me that moved was my hand. It reached and touched the butt of my Colt. Crunch. Crunch. Crunch. The sound of decomposed granite under booted heels. The voices of two men, slurred by drink. The flash of a flashlight.

"Over there, shee that truck?"

"Yeah, shure. You think I kin walk that far without fallin' flat on my fuckin' facesh?"

"You'll walk that far 'caush I got the fuckin' magazine."

"All right, all right! Shit, I tripped on a fuckin' rock! Let'sh do it right here."

"We need shomethin' to put the magazine on. Come on."

"Fuck. We shoulda put it on the hood of your truck."

"I don't wanna do it in front of fuckin' Jerry. He'sh alwaysh looking at my dick when I take a leak. Fuckin' makesh me nervous."

Laughter. "Alwaysh thought there was shomething fruity 'bout Jerry. Ever met his wife? She wears the pantsh in that family!"

"Probably wears more'n the pantsh. Big strap-on dildo and does it to him doggy-shtyle! Fuckin' Jerry shquealin' like a girl, 'Harder! Harder!'"

Laughter. More footfalls. The flashlight flashed over the hood of my Toyota, the beam bouncing through the cab window into the camper-shell, glancing over my sleeping bag. My pulse was pounding in my throat. I heard the rustle of glossy pages as the men laid their magazine on the hood. The truck lurched under me as one of them leaned against it.

"There we are!"

"Fuckin' shweet piece of cunt."

"My ballsh are about to burst."

I lay perfectly still as the men outside proceeded to jack off. With grunts and groans, they satisfied themselves. It didn't take long and soon they were zipping up and picking up their magazine. I lay there, barely daring to breathe, hoping they didn't take their flashlight and begin exploring the truck they had found parked by itself near the bank of the lake. They probably figured it belonged to some dedicated night-fisherman who had strolled down along the strand seeking a fisherman's wet-dream. Let's hope they're honest and not interested in burglarizing vehicles, I thought. Crunch. Crunch.

"Fuck, I needed that!" one of them said.

"What I need right now, ish a beer," said the other. Their crunching footfalls took them away.

I apologize to my reader for that last unattractive scene, but it is a perfect example of the shit that happened to me as I pursued these jobs far from home.

Things get pretty rank in No Woman's Land.

24

Running The Gauntlet
In which I have a typical morning on a new job

The gray light of dawn was a welcome thing.
Like Daniel, I had survived a night in the lion's den. Now I could rise,
shake off the night-fears and array myself for war in the accoutrement of
the construction worker. Cover my slick female skin with the worn
Levis and steel-toed boots, T-shirt with the sleeves cut off, showing my
well-defined deltoids, biceps and triceps, hard-earned proof of my
prowess as a laborer. Last night I was a woman alone cowering in the
dark, this morning I was a skilled laborer reporting for duty.

I knew what it would be like. It was always the same, showing
up among a crew of men who had never seen me before, much less ever
seen a female construction worker before. I braced myself for battle,
once more into the fray!

Driving away from the lake shore and into the closed
campground, I pulled up next to the office trailer under the pines,
parked and got out as if I had just driven in from home. Men were

arriving, parking their trucks and joining each other around the morning fire. Their eyes all turned to me as I walked towards the office.

Three short steps led to the office door. The foreman was coming down as I approached. "Good morning, sir," I said, sticking out my hand. "I'm Amy Farrell, Laborer." The foreman, a lean dark-haired fellow with a pitted face, who could've been cast as the head honcho bad guy in a John Wayne western, snorted at me. "Mack said he was sending me a girl," he said. "I expected a square-jawed bulldyke, not fuckin' Patty Loveless. Are you here to sing me a country song? How 'bout 'I'm That Kind Of Girl'? I like that one."

"No sir," I said, pulling my hand back when I saw he wasn't going to shake it. "I'm not here to sing. I'm here to work."

He snorted again. "And what sort of 'work' do you do?"

I heard sounds behind me. I heard a man say, "What's his problem with fuckin' Patty Loveless? I'd love to be fuckin' Patty Loveless, myself." Laughter, footfalls. The men had left the fire and were sauntering over.

I looked the foreman in the eye. "I'm a Union Laborer, sir. I can do anything."

Snorts. Laughter. A voice behind me said, "I wish she _was_ fuckin' Patty Loveless. There's something I'd like Patty to do for me."

Shit!" another man said. "There's somethin' I'd like Patty to do for me too but I'd be happy to crawl through a mile of concertina wire under enemy fire just to hear her fart through a field-phone." Guffaws of laughter.

"She wouldn't be Loveless if I had anything to do with it!" More laughter.

"Yeah, if you can call what you got Love!" Ha, Ha, Ha!

I looked around at the smirking faces. I had to remind myself that these men had wives and daughters, mowed their lawns on Saturday mornings, paid their taxes and voted in elections. At times like this, they seemed more like Mongol tribesmen, or just as bad, Mongol Motorcycle Club gang-members. Now completely circled by unknown hostile men, I waited for the foreman to decide what he was going to do. He could either send me home or he could put me to work. He put a hand into a pocket and pulled out a pack of Marlboros, flipping the hard pack open with a thumb and shaking up a cigarette. He slipped it between his thin lips and put the pack away. He stepped closer to me, eyeballing me as if sizing up a dog for the pit fights. Flicking a Bic, he lit up and blew smoke right in my face. Turning his head slightly but with his gaze locked on me, he spat a fleck of tobacco off his tongue.

"Mack said you're kick-ass," he said.

"I can kick any ass in this crowd," I said boldly. The way I figured it, I was gonna get sent home or put to work. If I got sent home it didn't matter who I insulted. If I was put to work, they'd see within an hour what I could do, and then any perceived insult wouldn't matter, the foreman would protect me because I was a valuable asset. Bosses are cheap, after all, they like to get their money's worth. I was a moneymaker, that was the bottom line.

"I'd like to see that," the foreman said, referring to me kicking any ass in the crowd. "Yes, indeed, I'd like to see that!"

I glanced about me, meeting a dozen pairs of unamused eyes. "Sure," I said, "where would you like me to start?"

The foreman gave a short barking laugh. He clamped a hand on my shoulder, his fingernails digging in. "Down, girl!" he said, and began steering me up the office steps. "You can start in my office." At the top step, he turned and looked at the men. "What're you guys fuckin' waiting for? Get to work!"

He kicked the door shut behind us. Once inside the closed office, he dropped his hand from my shoulder. I could feel the depressions his strong fingers had made in my skin. He moved away from me, stepping around his desk. A few catcalls sounded from outside and one loud holler of "Git some!" He slid some forms over his cluttered desk and tossed down a ball-point pen. "Where the hell did you get your moxie, Patty?" he said as he settled himself into a swivel-chair. "Don't mind if I call you that, do you?"

"Just born with it," I said, ignoring the Patty comment.

"Well, I'm gonna try you out for a day or two. You may turn out to be more trouble than you're worth."

"I'm not here for trouble, sir," I said. "I'm just here to make a living."

"Fuck, girl!" the man barked. "That's what they all say. Lemme tell ya something. Ain't too many girls got the balls to come out on a job like this, but every one I've seen's been more trouble'n she was worth. I got a project to wrap up and I'm late getting it done. Last thing I need is any trouble. Sign the papers, Patty, get to work and try to not to stir up any shit."

I signed the first one and handed it back. "What's this Ms. Construction?" I said, looking at the second form.

"Name of the company."

"I thought it was Randall and Sons," I said.

"Well, it is. And it ain't. See, they got this deal, minority-owned companies get to bid on these projects without having to beat out the competition. All that low-bid stuff, they can get around it. So, Randall and Sons starts a new company, only it's in the names of the wives, see? Same people, same equipment, different name. Companies do it all the time. Find a black guy and sign him up as owner of the company. Or a Mexican."

"Women aren't minorities," I said. "We're 51 percent of the population."

"Tell that to the federal government."

I signed the paper and handed it to him.

"My name's Jim," he said, shaking my hand. "How much do you weigh, anyhow?"

I smiled, wondering, what dangerous little job of work did he have in mind for the girl, the girl who was light as a feather? "One-twenty-five, give or take."

"Shit, Patty, I got cement sacks as heavy as that!"

"Where do ya want 'em stacked?" I said. "I'll get right on it."

Jim shook his head. "Help Tom load the Wacker-packer in the backhoe bucket and ride with him out to the job. He'll show ya what to do."

"All right," I said and went out the door. I found Tom at the Seatrain, the backhoe front bucket positioned at the big swing-open doors. I climbed up there and grabbed one of the handles and we swung the machine into the bucket. "I'm s'posed to ride to the job with you," I said.

"Sure, ride in the bucket and keep the Jumping Jack from falling out."

I stepped in and leaned against the mud-encrusted lip of the bucket, holding one hand on the compactor. I had seen these things carried in front buckets on many jobs and never had seen anyone riding along to hold onto them, but oh well. Normally when riding along on a backhoe, you climbed up next to the operator and sat on one of the wells of the huge rear wheels, holding on the grip handles. Some companies wouldn't let passengers ride on the heavy equipment, either on top or in the bucket, since it was an unsafe practice under OSHA standards.

Tom put the backhoe in gear and began moving it away from the Seatrain. He shifted from reverse to forward in a big lurch, almost tipping me out of the bucket. I glanced at him, thinking he must be a lousy operator. Maybe he was a laborer who had recently joined the Operator's Union as an apprentice. Even I could drive a backhoe smoother than that!

As we moved off through the forest, bouncing along dirt roads and pot-holed asphalt ones, Tom swerved the machine this way and that, ostensibly to avoid rough patches, but I soon noticed it seemed as if he were steering us into them rather than the other way around. Every time he bounced the backhoe into a dip and the unwieldy machine rocked back and forth, the Wacker-packer nearly toppled out but for my firm grip on it.

"Bumpy road!" Tom hollered over the engine noise.

"Let 'er buck!" I shouted back.

We hit a really big hole and the backhoe bounced and jerked. My feet left the surface with three inches of daylight between the soles of my boots and the steel of the bucket. The Wacker bounced and almost flew forward. I regained my footing and threw my weight against the Wacker, pushing it back in place. I glared at Tom.

"Ride 'em, cowgirl!" he hollered. I was sure he wanted me to ask him to slow down, but I'd rather be dumped out of the bucket with a hundred and eighty pounds of compactor on top of me than do that.

"Yee Haw!" was all I said. We came clattering up to the job site, the backhoe lurching, Tom bouncing up and down on his operator's seat, me clinging to the bucket lip with one hand and the compactor with the other, with the Wacker's metal foot rattling and clanging up and down.

All eyes turned towards us as Tom shut the machine down. I waited a beat for him to lower the bucket to the ground so we could unload the compactor but he just sat there. I jumped down (it was about two feet) and, grasping the handle on one side of the Wacker, I gave it a hard yank, stepping back to get my feet out of the way as the thing hit the ground with a thud. I had jerked these unwieldy beasts around on jobs before and I knew how to handle them. This was the first time I had unloaded one from two feet off the ground, however. I heard a collective intake of breath from the men behind me. They had expected me to break my foot with the thing or else dump it sideways on the ground. It had landed perfectly. "Thanks, Tom!" I said cheerfully, relieved that it had gone so well.

"Did ya like your ride?" Tom asked.

"Best mechanical bull ride I ever had!" I said.

Tom started the machine. "We'll do it again tonight!"

"Can't wait!" I shouted.

I glanced around me at the work site, saw the familiar sight of a trench stretching away into the woods, several lengths of pipe laid, fine dirt spread loosely over what had to be other pipe invisible under the soil. I had been here before! I flicked a choke switch on the Wacker, pulled the cord hard, once, twice and thrice. The motor started, coughing blue smoke out a port on the side. I thumbed the choke switch slowly shut, let it warm up for a few seconds and gave the machine some gas. As it revved, it began to bounce and bump around. These machines weren't called Jumping Jacks for nothing! I had to hold onto it or it would fall over. I was glad I had my steel-toed boots on.

These things can really nail you if you're not careful!

As the motor sped up, the compactor began to move. I walked behind it, steering it with side-to-side and front-to-back pressure on the handles. I brought it to the edge of the trench and glanced down. The trench was about four feet deep. I could do this the easy way (the OSHA-approved way!), shut the Wacker down and ask for help lowering it into the trench, or I could do it the cool way, the way Dutch had once shown me. The way Dutch had made an impression on every man on the crew. The way that made a statement. The statement was: I'm a By-God-Laborer, don't fuck with me!

Of course I went for the statement. I revved the Wacker-packer hard and went straight for the edge. This would either work and look really cool or this would dump me ass-over-teakettle into the trench with a compactor on top of me!

I shot the machine over the edge, tipping it back slightly so its foot would land as far forward as possible without it falling backwards. As it dropped into the trench I bent my body in half and followed it, my feet hitting the ground only a split second after its big metal foot struck home. Fwump! My hands on either side-handle, I braced the thing until it got its equilibrium and in a second my compactor and I were compacting our way down the trench as if we'd always been there. I felt male eyes on my back but I knew what to do and I just kept doing it. Do the work. No one can fault if you just do the work.

Pretty soon the crew was in the trench with me, just doing the work. I made sure no one got their hands on that Wacker-packer all day and when Tom pulled his backhoe close to the trench lip at the end of the day, he and another man helped me load it into the bucket for the ride back to the Seatrain. On the ride back, Tom went along as gentle as a pony.

Step one, show 'em you can do the work.

25

Good Dog Lacy
In which my dog saves my sanity if not my life

On Friday at the end of the day, Jim handed out the paychecks. I received my first Ms. Construction check and gave a wry smile. I was still amused by the company name. The men were making crass jokes about it, sashaying around with limp wrists and lisping at one another. "I work for Mith Consthruction, who do you work for, Handthome?"

"Thay, Thailor, ith thith the work thite of Mith Consthruction?"

"Yeth ith ith. Do you have a job you wanth uth to do?"

"Yeth, I need thome holeth dug."

"Well, you came to the right plathe. Our menth know all abouth holeth."

I walked away from the antics of the rest of the crew and asked Jim, "Boss, you planning on shit-canning me any time soon?"

Jim smirked at me and said, "Now, Patty, why would I wanna shit-can you?"

I shrugged. "No reason, I just wonder if I can bring my trailer up here."

The three-plus hour drive was a bitch. To arrive at seven, I was leaving home at four in the morning. After that first night sleeping in the truck I had gone home every night, not wanting to take my chances with the hunters on the lakeside.

"No problem, you can be our night guard. We've had some break-ins."

"Can I bring my dog?"

"Sure, bring Bowser if you want."

"Her name's Lacy," I said.

Jim gave his trademark snort. "Poodle?"

"No, Australian Shepherd."

"Oh, that's good. Lacy sounded foofy."

"It's like Cagney and Lacy," I clarified, referring to a popular TV show about tough women cops.

"Sure, girly, whatever you want. Bring your trailer, bring your dog. Bring the fuckin' wife and kids, whatever you want!" He disappeared into the office.

The following Sunday I pulled my twelve-foot trailer up to the site and set it up across from the Seatrain and office trailer. Lacy and I made ourselves at home.

Lacy was hands-down the best dog that ever was, bar none. I'd bet my bottom dollar and swear on a stack of Bibles. Can't prove it but I know it and you can't convince me otherwise, that's all there is to it. For one thing, she came out of the mountains, which is as good an endorsement as you're likely to find. Second, she's the only dog I know that flew in a helicopter, which is pretty neat, if nothing else. But mainly, she was the most loyal, devoted and steadfast dog I've ever known, which is something considering that her species is known for its loyalty, devotion and steadfastness. She was also easy on the eyes, by which I mean she was a pretty thing, peach all over with a cream ruff, white paws and chest, long silky coat and bright light-brown eyes with a tiny pearl spot in one of them. People everywhere would hurry on over when they saw me with her, saying, "Is that your dog? She is so beautiful!" Veterinarians would fawn over her and practically treat her for free. Practically.

Cowboys offered me real money for her, because she was cowy and they liked her smart look. Never knew a cowboy that didn't like fine things. They don't tend to have much, but what they do have is fine.

She died in 1999 and all dogs I've had since have been judged on the Lacy scale of 1-10. Lacy was an 11, of course. She came to me by a curious path, having been flown out of the snowy back country on a rescue helicopter in the dead of winter. If I hadn't walked into Donna Ride's feed store in Three Rivers that Monday at noon, the best dog in the world might have gone to someone else. As it was, when I walked into the feed store for no good reason, I found Donna and Martha Jameson sitting on feed sacks, Donna holding the leash of a filthy, matted, sooty, tick-ridden, flea-bitten skeleton of a dog. "Where'd you get that funny-looking dog?" I asked Donna.

Donna had flashed her dazzling big-toothed smile and said, "Martha here brought it down from Ash Mountain."

Martha looked at me. Her long reddish hair fell down her back to her waist. She worked in Sequoia National Park in the Fire Office at the Ash Mountain headquarters. "Found her tied to a bush, shivering and shaking this morning. Brought her into my office and warmed the poor thing up. Called around and got the whole story." I took a feed sack and held out my hand to the skinny dog. She sniffed, then licked my hand. "What is the whole story?"

"Search and rescue operation last week," Martha said, "for those lost skiers?"

"Heard about that," I said.

"Snow storm dumped three feet on the rescue team, so they made it to one of the back country huts. When they got there, they found it already occupied."

"The lost skiers?"

"No, an old guy named Tyrone Fields. They had been looking for him for years. He's kind of a tramp, a homeless guy, only he lives in the mountains. He survives by breaking into people's cabins and eating up all their stores, burning all their firewood and so on. They had warrants on him in four counties."

"That's a new one," Donna said.

"Well," Martha elaborated, "it seems this guy's father or grandfather used to be the superintendent of Sequoia Park and as a boy this fellow spent all his summers in the back country. Knows it like you know the neighborhood you grew up in. Considers it his home turf."

"Amazing," I said, wondering where the scruffy-looking dog came in.

"So this was his dog?" Donna queried.

"She was with him, sharing his predicament," Martha said. "They were snowed in, all the food in the cabin was gone, the firewood burnt up and he was breaking up the furniture and burning it for warmth. The rangers were pissed as hell when they got there and found nothing but an empty shell. But they were glad to catch Fields red-handed. They arrested him and once the storm broke, had him flown out in a helicopter and some food and supplies flown in. They found the skiers and evacuated everyone off the mountain."

"The dog too," I said, rubbing the dog's sooty ears.

"Not at first," Martha said. "They didn't have room. They left her there by herself one more night and sent a copter in to get her the next day, Friday. They tied her to a bush out in front of the Fire Office and called Animal Control to come get her. That was Friday afternoon, late, the way I heard it. She was still there this morning when I came to work."

"Poor thing!" I said.

"She's been through hell," Donna agreed.

"Well, a few people got a piece of my mind, I tell you," Martha said. "My boss was surprised the dog was still there. He said, 'Let me call Animal Control again.' I said, 'What's gonna happen to her?' He said, 'Her owner's going to jail for a long time so she'll be humanely disposed of.' I said, 'Well, consider her already humanely disposed of, boss, 'cause I ain't gonna let her be put down.' He said, 'if anybody asks me, I'll say we called Animal Control on Friday and that's the last I saw of that dog.' I said, 'You wouldn't be lying.' Then as soon as my lunch rolled around I got her out of there!"

Donna said, "I'll take care of her until you get off work. I'll feed her, bathe her and groom her. Amy can help, right, Amy?"

"Sure," I said. "Look, she's got big fuzzy clown feet!"

"That's from being in the snow so much," Donna said. "She's grown all the fur to keep her feet warm."

Martha looked at her watch. "I gotta get back."

"You won't recognize her when you see her next!" Donna called after her.

By the time Donna and I had bathed, flea-dipped, de-ticked, de-matted, brushed and nail-clipped the dog, she was a totally different animal. "She's gorgeous!" Donna said. "Oh baby, I wish I had papers on you!" Donna was a breeder and trainer of Champion Australian Shepherds. Donna had me hold the dog steady while she carefully ran the electric clippers all around the fuzzy paws, buzzing off the long snowshoe fur and trimming between each toe.

"That's better," Donna said. "Much more ladylike than those big clodhoppers! And you are a pretty little lady, aren't you?"

The dog licked Donna's face and wagged her body. "Her tail's docked, so she came from a breeder originally," Donna remarked.

"I wonder how this Tyrone guy got her?" I said.

"Found her, stole her, who knows?" Donna said. "One thing, he couldn't have been too bad a man, to make such a sweet dog. You can tell a lot about a person by their dog."

Halfway through the grooming, I had already started wanting this dog. She was so patient and so gentle, considering all the tugging, scrubbing, pinching and pulling we were doing on her. Donna, a professional dog-groomer was amazed the dog didn't bite or growl or give us any trouble. "She's really sweet-tempered!" Donna kept saying. Groomed and blow-dried, the beautiful peach-colored pooch stood there gleaming in the light that came in through the front windows of the feed store.

"She's really pretty," Donna said. "This is an unusual color variation in the red-tri Aussie. It's a recessive gene that produces this peach. Very special, though not exactly breed standard."

"I don't mind," I blurted, and Donna smiled at me.

"Well, baby, let's see if you know anything." Donna took up the leash and began doing obedience moves with the dog. Donna was an obedience class trainer.

"No, she doesn't know anything, but she learns really quick." Pretty soon, Donna had the dog heeling like a competition dog, doing half-turns and quarter turns, and staying in a down-stay with the leash dropped in front of her while Donna came and sat beside me on the feed sack. "Really great!" Donna enthused. "With a little training, I predict that dog could be winning blue ribbons."

"You should do it," I said.

"Oh, I can't use her," Donna said. "No papers. If I can't breed 'em, I don't need 'em!"

"I want her," I said.

Donna threw her arm across my shoulders and gave me that winning smile. "We'll see what Martha has in mind for her." Then she winked at me.

Turned out it wasn't Martha that needed convincing to let me have the dog, it was my partner Angie.

While I have always had an affinity for critters of all kinds since my earliest remembrances, Angie had never been an animal person. I had already brought home a feral cat I had tamed while living lonely at the KOA Kampground during horseshoeing school, a lovely calico I had named Josie after one that my mother had owned during my early childhood. Mom's Josie, named for Joseph's coat of many colors, had earned fame in our family lore for having a litter of multicolored kittens on Easter morning which had been discovered in a garden nest by my siblings during an Easter egg hunt, and amazingly, my Josie did the exact same thing on Easter morning 1986. Angie had tolerated my mystical cat from the KOA because the feline brought me comfort when I had just lost my father, but she wasn't exactly thrilled about a dog.

It was the first serious argument I remember she and I having. First of what would prove to be many.

Martha, a Yellow Labrador breeder and trainer, was often away at dog shows and, at the urging of Donna, had asked Angie (whom she knew from work) if we would might dog-sit the peach-colored Aussie while she was away on some weekends. Grudgingly, Angie had said we would. The first weekend, while Angie was sitting on the couch, the dog approached her. "I'm not that into you," Angie said blandly. To her surprise, the dog abruptly stopped, turned and walked as far away as she could and lay down, her head in the opposite direction. She crossed her front paws one over the other, like a little lady.

"Well, one thing I have to admit," Angie stated, "she is very polite. And look at the way she crosses her legs!"

It was that politeness which won her over at last. Lacy, as I called the canine, was so very well-mannered that everyone, even people who didn't like dogs, liked her. As far as Angie was concerned, if she had to have a dog around (and sooner or later, living with me, she would) it might as well be a quiet, pretty, well-mannered dog. Soon after it was official, I signed Lacy and me up for one of Donna's obedience classes. As predicted, Lacy was a natural and she won the top grade in the class of twelve.

Whenever I could, I took Lacy with me on my jobs. On most jobs it just wasn't allowed, but on some mountain jobs I was able to take her. She would spend the day tied to a tree near my work area, or else tied up outside my trailer in the man-camp or even inside my trailer. At my lunch breaks I would walk her and toss a tennis ball or a stick. At Shaver Lake when I camped alone on the Ms. Construction job, I don't know that I could have done it without her. I never spent another night there without both Lacy and my loaded Colt.

I had thought Jim was teasing me when he said I could be the night-guard, but sure enough, one dark night I woke to hear Lacy's low growl. Shushing her and listening hard, I heard muffled voices outside. I crept from my bed and peered out through the front windows of my trailer. Over by the Seatrain, flashlights zagged about and I could make out several figures. There were men trying to break into the lock-up!

155

I put my feet into my boots and reached under my pillow for my Colt. I undid the latch of the trailer door, slipping my hand through Lacy's collar. "All right, girl," I whispered and stepped outside, keeping the trailer between me and men. I held tight to the dog and hunkered down next to the side of the tongue, where I could peer around but where I would not be seen.   One man was swinging a sledge-hammer, trying to break the padlocks that held the big lever-latches on the container box shut. Three other men were standing back, waiting to swing the big doors open and steal the expensive equipment inside.

A fifth man was walking toward my trailer, his flashlight scanning my shuttered windows. A shiver went down my back that had nothing to do with the mountain chill.

I placed my mouth next to Lacy's ear and said in a gruff voice, "Go get 'em, Spike! Get 'em!" Lacy exploded into ferocious snarling and barking. "Get 'em! Get 'em!" I said to urge her on. I held her collar so she could not actually run over there, but the men heard her and froze. I fired off one round from the Colt, aiming at the ground some feet away, nowhere near the men. The sound was a sharp Crack! that made my ears ring. The burglars bolted. "Go get 'em! Get 'em!" I yelled gruffly and Lacy kept up the horrible snarling and barking. The men climbed into a van that was idling nearby with its headlights out and kicked up dust as they drove away.

"Good girl, Lacy!" I praised her.

The get 'em trick was one she must have been taught by Tyrone Fields. I had discovered it by chance one day while throwing balls for her. She had missed the first ball and to make her find it, I had thrown the second ball after it. "Go get 'em!" I had shouted, thinking as smart as she was, she might pick up both and bring them back to me. But as soon as she heard "Get 'em!" she broke into a furious snarling, growling and barking. It startled me, and Angie, standing nearby, said, "That dog's gone crazy!" But I tried it again and found that it was as if she had been trained to the response. I saw also how useful it could be.

If I felt threatened, I could squat down next to her, whisper those magic words into her ear, get her started with the snarling and barking and then, holding on to her collar, I'd say to the threatening person, "I don't know if I can hold on to her, you had better back away!" Lacy would even oblige by jumping up against the leash or collar as if she would charge the person if I let go of her.

It was mostly a game to her, for which she'd be praised, but I knew from the serious way she pulled on the collar, that if I ever was seriously threatened, Lacy wouldn't hold back.

My dog would fight for me.

Amy R Farrell

26

She-bolts And Mule Pussies
In which I break the bonds of ladylike behavior once and for all

The Ms. Construction crew was pretty hard-core.

In fact, if they were an entire crew of ironworkers they couldn't have been any worse. They cussed a blue streak, farted and burped all through lunch, hocked and spat, recounted in gross detail their sexual conquests, rubbed their crotches in front of me and pissed on tree trunks in plain view. Men would argue and threaten one another, even go to pushing and shoving while others would egg them on. Jim, the foreman, was moody and volatile; hard to predict from one day to the next. Men would get shit-canned and others would appear on the job. I never knew when it might happen to me, so I took each day as it came.

I had my own list of rules for making it in No Woman's Land and I repeated them to myself like little mantras throughout the day: Do what you're told to do; don't get bucked off; don't let 'em take your tools; never grovel; be a moneymaker; do the work; be ready for anything that comes down the trench; don't get your feelings hurt; pick up any glove you're thrown. And be ready to move on at a moment's notice!

Like rodbusters, these guys took sexual harassment to a high degree. Maybe they thought they could tramp me off the job, or maybe they thought I'd be the crew whore. More than once, when walking off into the woods for a private place to pee, one of the guys would tail me, hoping at least to see my ass, or at most to get a piece of it. Like with Breezy, I had to shove my way past more than one man to get safely back to work. "I can't believe it," one guy said as I passed him, "you really do piss squatting down!"

"Watch all you like," I said, "but you lay a hand on me, I'll knock you down." When they realized that actual sex wasn't going to happen on the job, some of the men decided that sexual innuendo would be a sorry yet acceptable alternative. They pulled out all the stops.

I decided to fight fire with fire. I wanted to make it clear that they could not embarrass me, that I had heard it all before and then some. If they had any delusions that I was some kind of naive girl-next-door with the sensibilities of a virgin, well, they had another delusion coming.

At least it was a war I felt I could win, or at least, hold my own.

"What're you having her do?" one of the men asked Jim one morning, as I was strapping on my tool belt after receiving my orders.

"She's gonna go set those walers." Jim said. Walers are 2x4 boards set horizontally to brace up plywood cement forms.

"Maybe I can go too," the man sneered, catching my eye. "I'd sure like to whale her!"

I glanced at his crotch, and sneered back, "Wouldn't have much luck with that little minnow."

Another time I was holding the end of a guy's tape measure while he ran it out to measure something. "Give me a couple inches," I said.

"Oh, I'll give you more than a couple inches!" he offered, lasciviously.

I glanced over and said, "You'll need more'n a two-inch tape measure."

One day, while working with a guy who kept making sexual comments, I said, "I feel sorry for you men. You're just slaves to your dicks. Don't you realize it's all just hormones?"

The guy grinned at me. "Yeah, and don't I love to hear a whore moan!"

I said, "I bet they all moan when they see you coming with a twenty-dollar bill!"

And so it went, one comment after another, all day, every day.

All the usual construction slang was bantered about, and then some! Donkey dongs and vibrators, male and female ends of pipe being slipped together ("fits together like me and you," one guy would always say when we joined two lengths of pipe, "especially after you lube it up a little!"), digging holes and filling holes, screwing and screwdrivers, big and little hammers, lubed she-bolts and mule pussies!

She-bolts are large bolts that are heavily greased then slid into steel concrete forms to hold the forms at a set width, adjusted by the turning of the large nuts and spaced by a metal sheath that stays inside of the concrete once the forms are stripped. The very act of prepping she-bolts (sitting in a circle with a bunch of guys dipping your hand into a bucket of grease and smearing it over a large bolt then sliding the bolt into its sheath) is sexually-charged and ripe for comment.

"Mule pussies" are snaptie wedges, convex metal plates with a hole and slot in them, designed so that the button-end of a metal snaptie goes through the hole and slides down the slot to its proper adjustment on the convex surface of the wedge. If you've see looked under a female horse's tail you'll know why they're called mule pussies. Snapties run through the concrete form and when pinned in place with the wedge hold the walers in place so that when wet mud is pumped and vibrated into place the plywood form stays rigid. When the forms are stripped, the snapties break off below the concrete surface (hence their name) and the little cone-shaped holes they leave are filled with dry-patch cement. Even the term to "strip" forms was in invitation for sex talk.

For each and every tool, method and material used on the job there were several different ways it could be used as a sexual comment.

In trying to ward off the barbarians, I regret to say I increased the count.

27

Kick Ass

In which I up the ante

"**Kick-ass,** over here a minute!" Jim hollered one morning as I stood near the Seatrain to help load tools into the loader bucket. The Patty-shit had finally worn off and I had a new nickname.

I walked over to the office steps. "What is it, boss?"

Jim scowled and spat on the ground. "I gotta problem where to put you today."

Now I scowled too. Where to put me had never been a problem before. We had pipeline to lay, galvanized culverts to set across roadways, drain inlets to build, concrete pads for water tanks to construct and restrooms to demolish and rebuild. In the preceding weeks, I had worked on pretty much all of it and not a single job had bucked me off. There hadn't been a conflict with any of the guys that I hadn't handled, without taking more shit than I had coming to me and without licking any boots.

"Excuse me for asking, boss, but why is there a problem?"

Jim glanced over towards the men and lowered his voice. "See, I gotta decide which crew needs to speed it up," he said. "Whoever I put you with works harder so they don't get shown up by a girl, so every day I gotta decide who needs speeding up the most."

This explained a lot. With several different projects going on at once, I found myself moved from one to the next with regularity. Thinking back on it, it now seemed that I got moved around more than the other workers. Now I knew why.

"What do you think?" Jim asked. I realized that Jim was letting me in on this so that I could advise him. "They all work harder when they see me coming," he went on, "so I try to hide from 'em but I figure, you see 'em as they are when I'm not around. So what do you think?"

I looked over at the men. They were going in and out of the Seatrain, carrying shovels, picks, rakes, and buckets full of hand-tools. Watching them, all their little personalities flashing in their smiles and gestures, it all came clear to me.

"Fonzie is your slowest guy," I said. He was called that because he was always combing his dark hair back with a straight comb he kept in his back pocket (why a guy bothered to comb his hair all day then cram a hard hat on it, I'll never understand), like the character on the TV show "Happy Days."

"He thinks it's funny to milk every job for all its worth," I added, because the guy had said as much to me.

Jim snorted. "I thought so. He's the owner's nephew so I can't shit-can him. Why don't you work on his crew today and see if you can make him look bad?"

"That won't be hard," I said.

Jim grinned like a crocodile. "Make him look real bad, and then encourage the other guys to mock him. Maybe that'll shake him up."

"Sure boss," I said.

"Couple days with Fonzie, then we'll talk again about where you're needed next." He pawed in his pocket for his smokes.

"Sure," I said, looking at the men. "I got some ideas."

Jim lit up a cigarette and blew smoke at me. "Sic 'em, kid."

Shifted around from crew to crew, acting as an inside agent for the job boss, waging a war of words and wit with the Mongols, fending off unwanted sexual advances, working twice as fast as anyone just to keep them on their toes, pulling night-guard duty at night, and sleeping scared in a 12-foot trailer in the deep forest with drunken deer-hunters whooping it up all around me, and would-be burglars looking for a pay-day, I was getting a little frazzled!

Lacy had to stay cooped up in the trailer all day. I let her out and chucked a tennis ball for her during my lunch breaks, which meant I didn't even get to sit down and eat my lunch, so I was on my feet all day. The Laborer's Union agreement states that each worker gets a half hour break for every five hours of work, consequently there are no breaks other than a half hour for lunch on union construction jobs, even when working ten hour days. These jobs are about making money, not mollycoddling employees. Bosses are cheap, they will only give you what you got coming.

By the end of a ten hour day, I was pretty beat. But I still had obligations. Lacy needed a long walk and I needed to call home. Angie wanted to hear from me each day, to make sure I was still alive and hadn't disappeared into the ether, to become a cold case in a missing persons file. Which, considering the conditions of my existence at Shaver Lake, was distinctly possible.

This was before the days of cellular phones, so I had to perch at one of the few working pay phones near the lake and shift from foot to foot trying to stay warm while we talked. Once the sun went over, it got damned cold at seven thousand feet elevation in the Sierra Nevada. The stiff steel-wrapped cord of the pay phone was only two feet long so I couldn't even sit on the ground but had to stand (more time on my feet!) while Angie described her day and complained about being left home with all the responsibilities of housekeeping and caring for a small child (Angie had given birth to Daniel in August of 1988). I supposed that male construction workers heard all about it too! Or maybe not.

Maybe the wives of male construction workers didn't expect any different. She would put Daniel on to talk to me. Between the two of them, sometimes the phone calls went on for forty-five minutes to an hour. I would be frozen solid by the time Angie would hang up. I figured it was the least I could do not to cut it short. My absentee parent guilt was aroused. I had had an absentee parent in my father, gone for business trips and deep into his workaholism and alcoholism. I didn't want to make Pop's mistakes with my own family.

Hands in the pockets of my Carhartt jacket, my old battered Resistol cowboy hat on my head, my hair still in its braid from the work day, after hanging up the phone, Lacy and I would take a long hitch through the darkening forest towards the lake. The dog would run out ahead of me, her nose to the ground, chasing a late bird or a dusk-forging squirrel, then come bounding back to my side. The pine scent in my nostrils, the crunch of little fir cones under my work boots, the pink light of early evening turning the forest floor golden, I would walk a circuitous path between granite boulders and fallen logs, wending my way towards the dark blue water.

Busting out of the forest onto the lake-side, Lacy and I would crunch our way over the decomposed granite sand to where the water lap-lapped against the shore, a cold breeze pushing it. Lacy would splash into the shallows and lick up water, then bound back onto the dry and give herself a shake and take off running after some duck she saw nested down in a tangle of driftwood, causing it to raise with a clap of pinions into the coming-night sky. She'd come running back, all pleased with herself and I would squat down and hug her to me. A delicate lick on the face, just one, would be my reward and Lacy would be off again. A thrown stick, another duck, a piece of flotsam bobbing at water's edge, all would captivate her. It made me smile to watch her. The world was good when Lacy was happy!

And though I was exhausted, these capers in the dusk were a welcome end to my days. My back, my legs, my feet and my shoulders burned with the hard labor of the job, but my mind cast off its fatigue as Lacy raced in pursuit of a coot.

On our rambles, I avoided the parts of the lake where easy access drew the hunters with their four-wheelers, beer coolers and guns, but if I had to walk the gauntlet, I'd tuck my braid inside my coat, turn my collar up, pull my hat brim down and feel solace in the lump of my

Colt under my coat as I tried to walk like a man through the trees. Right now, that's what I wanted them to see, a man among men. Someone who pissed standing up.

In the dim light that is probably what they did see. A mountain man: Strong; capable; confident; walking his dog in the early hours of the night. Balls of brass. Don't fuck with me.

Arriving back at the trailer in the full darkness of evening, I'd unlock and let us in, latching the door behind us. Lighting my single Kerosene lamp, I'd feed Lacy her can of Pedigree and I'd paw through the cupboard for my vegetarian chili or Campbell's Chunky Vegetable Soup. The trailer would be chill inside and I'd light the gas oven and leave the door cracked open with an empty soup can to warm the small space. Lacy would curl up on my bed and watch me with her gentle eyes until they fanned shut, her long lashes like moth wings, and she was asleep.

Eating soup out of the pot, dipping bread into it, I'd read tales of Arthur's knights or Jesse James' rogues from dog-eared books, and thus I'd spend the hours until bedtime.

Six-shooter under my pillow, I'd sleep uneasy, one ear listening out for the sound of burglars or barbarians.

With a good dog at my feet.

Amy R Farrell   .

28

Ms. Construction
In which I am what I am

One early morning, Manny, one of the biggest assholes on the job, drove into the job site honking his horn and shouting out his truck window. He pulled up to the tongue of my trailer and pushed his bumper against it, rocking my little house to and fro, almost knocking it off its stands. "Hey, girl, get up! Come see what I got for ya!"

It was about five-forty-five a.m. and I was already up, getting ready to make my breakfast and have time to walk Lacy before the work day started at seven. I pulled back the curtain at the front of the trailer and peered out. Directly outside my window in the early morning gray light, lay a dead deer, rivulets of dark blood running from its gaping mouth. It was a six-point buck tied down on the hood of Manny's F-250, its sleek flank stained red and its tongue lolling out.

"Ah, Jesus!" I uttered in disgust.

"Come on out, girl! Take a look!" Manny hollered, revving his engine and rocking my trailer back and forth. Lacy was already growling and now she started to bark. "Go away, Manny!" I shouted, glaring through the dusty window at his smirking face.

"Not 'til you come out here!" he shouted. "I want you to see this buck I got last night!" He left his truck pushed against my trailer, opened his door and climbed out.

"Shit!" I said, not wanting him to come to the door. I reached for the latch and stepped outside.

"Come on out!" Manny shouted as I stepped out. Lacy shot past me and darted straight for Manny. She leaped into the air and struck his chest with her front feet, all her weight driving into him. The snarl that issued from between her bared teeth chilled my blood. Manny staggered back. Lacy landed on her feet, circled around behind me and leaped for Manny again. She bounced on him in exactly the same manner, staggering him back again. Manny's look of horror was priceless. I almost laughed.

He regained his balance and backpedaled for his open truck door. "Get her off me!" he shouted, reaching into the cab for his rifle. "Get her off me or I'll shoot her!" He drew the long gun and fumbled with the bolt.

"Lacy, come!" I ordered sharply, and the well-trained dog broke off her attack and came instantly, sitting in front of me.

"I'll fuckin' shoot that fuckin' dog!" Manny was yelling, his rifle pointed at Lacy.

"You will not shoot my dog, you bastard!" I shouted back. "What the hell do you expect her to do, with you acting that way? You come at me like you're attacking me, all aggressive and smelling of blood! What kind of dog would she be if she didn't attack you?"

Manny's face changed ever so slightly but he didn't lower his rifle.

"You're just lucky she only pushed you and didn't rip your face off!"

"I'll shoot her if she ever does it again," he threatened.

"I'll shoot you if you shoot my dog," I said, low like a growl.

Manny's eyes met mine. He could see I wasn't shitting him. He lowered his rifle. He turned and put the gun back on the truck seat. "Well, anyway," he said, "I wanted you to see the buck I got last night."

"I saw it plenty good from the window," I said, coolly.

"Yeah, well, you shoulda seen it," he bragged. "Shot through thick cover at a hundred yards, one shot."

"Okay, fine," I said, trying to cut off the good-old-boy patter. I wasn't in the mood for the lets-pull-em-out-and-measure-em game. Let him play it with the guys when they showed up! "You're the great white hunter. You're a real killer. Deer fear you. Your balls are bigger than mine." I turned to go.

"What?" Manny said. "What kinda bullshit is that?"

I reached the door to my trailer and looked back at him. "My dog's better than your dog," I said as a parting shot.

"I don't have a fuckin' dog!" Manny shouted.

"Your loss." I shrugged, stepped inside and closed the door.

Lacy stood beside me, her body pressed against my calf. "Thanks, girl," I said softly. "Go lie down." The dog gave a little huff and jumped up on the bed. I peeked out the front window. Manny stood beside his truck, kicking at the front tire. He looked at his dead deer and his shoulders slumped. He looked like a guy who had just tried to make friends with a pro ball player and been rebuffed. I realized in a flash that he had been trying to impress me. If I had been a guy living in the man-camp, he would have done exactly the same thing.

He looked up and saw me watching him. "All right, I'm sorry!" he shouted.

I sighed and smiled at him. Stupid jerk, I thought. "Apology accepted," I shouted back through the glass. He nodded, got into his truck and backed it away from my trailer. A little while later he had a fire going in the camp circle where the men all gathered before work in the morning. Lacy and I came out of the trailer, me holding my coffee mug and a plate of toast. I sat on a rock with Lacy at my heel. Manny had his Thermos and we drank coffee together in silence until the other men arrived.

To Manny's pleasure, <u>they</u> were all duly impressed with his murdered deer. Manny smirked at me over the nodding heads of his fellow males. They at least, knew the proper response to a successful hunt! Admittedly, my upbringing among men like my father had not prepared me for what I had to deal with here in No Woman's Land.

Pop hadn't exactly been the Great White Hunter.

Soon the snow flew and the layoffs came. I hauled my trailer out of Shaver Lake and took up my winter mantle as full-time stay-at-home mom to Daniel and partner to Angie. The next summer would find me on other as-of-yet-unknown jobs, but the winter was a time to regroup and focus on family and the community in which I lived, the town of Three Rivers. And to reflect upon my life, where I had come from and where I was headed.

Looking back on the Ms. Construction job, it seems a turning point in my construction career. Four years of experience under my well-worn tool-belt, I had earned my own reputation in my union hall and on the jobs. I was known as kick-ass and reliable, a real moneymaker. I had learned from men like Placido, Juan and Dutch the toughness and tenacity that make a good construction worker. I had survived attempts on my life by assholes like Randy, warded off sexual assault by creeps like Breezy and I had learned how to live and work with pushy aggressive jerks like Manny. I had seen that, as rough around the edges as these men were, they were the people who built America. Their will, their straining muscles, their calloused hands, their skill with tools, their practical knowledge of how things go together in the real world of rock and steel, dirt and concrete, wood and nail, flesh and bone.

In the realm of realities, nothing gets done without men like these. Where the people of the mind are paper tigers, these guys are the real thing. I had gone from a half-pitying contempt for them to a true heartfelt respect.

By grasping a thread that had led me into a world where few women had ever gone, I had faced whatever beasts might dwell there, but I was a beast too. I had come unbidden, penetrated the private lair they shared only with other men. I should never have expected a warm greeting on the sacred ground of male initiation and when I reflected on it honestly, my initiation wasn't a whole lot different than that which they gave each other. Mine was simply geared towards challenging my particular weakness, that of being female. All rituals of initiation are designed to challenge you, see what you are made off, see if you will become one of the tribe or if you will cut and run.

Ed and Jody Farrell didn't raise no quitters, so I had not cut and run, and in time, I had made a place for myself in the tribe. None of the men had liked it at first, and many would never accept it, but there were a few that finally embraced me like a brother. The common bond of shared sweat and hardship meant more than could (or would) ever be expressed. As a woman, I had to let go of wanting them to say it, but they probably liked me more than they would admit, even to themselves. I suppose the same could be said of me, as regards them.

The days up on Shaver Lake were hard, the nights were scary and I was lonely. I would have been lost without my dog. But I'll always remember the sun going over the ridge and casting a pink glow over the cold lake waters. I'll always remember the smell of wood smoke in my nostrils and the chill wind blowing across the water. The chorus of coyotes on the far bank and Orion the Warrior rising in the east and straddling the ridge-tops. The dark stoic pines lining the shore and the path through them to my trailer door. Lacy racing a low-flying duck along the strand. Walking with confidence and well-armed among the men of the mountain, my cowboy hat hiding my true nature. Or maybe not. Maybe what they saw of me was just what I was.

What I had grown to be, living and working among the men. Strong, capable, confident.

Maybe it was more than just a stupid company name after all, maybe it was what I had become:

Ms. Construction.

Amy R Farrell

PART FOUR:

ROCK AND A HARD PLACE

From the silent womb he came. Clamoring, his new voice

rang. After thirty-seven years... I saw him in to death.

Silently he left. Just the closing of his eyes... a final breath.

This time the cries... were mine.

--Jody Farrell, 1989

Amy R Farrell

29

Family Of Origin
In which I reflect on whence I came

My parents always considered themselves to be citizens of the world, members of a broader family. They raised all of their children to perceive the interconnectedness of all living beings and to respect the earth as our home and as a nurturing mother. My mother was a perfect example to me of how to raise my own child. She lived her principals daily and never wavered in what she believed in. While my father's public activism and civil service was noted in newspaper articles and television interviews, my mother's efforts were quieter, played close to the vest. While my father mounted his steed every day and rode off to slay the dragon, my mother was quietly saving the world at home.

Jody Oppermann had grown up in a Michigan family of German-descent. The Oppermanns were a family of well-to-do business-owners, newspaper editors, architectural engineers and entrepreneurs, pillars of the Saginaw community. The family business,

Oppermann's Fur Company, founded after the Civil War by my mother's great-grandfather Frederick C. Oppermann, had for generations been a source of pride as well as a means of support for the family. During the Great Depression, the fur company went out of business and the family which had lived in comfort and ease fell on hard times. My mother, a child at the time, witnessed the adults in her life struggling with the changes that a lowered social status wrought on the proud Teutonic nature.

In a family that repressed displays of emotion, young Jody learned to gain approval through obedience and quiescence. She was not a brilliant student nor a member of the most popular clique at school but a sweet-natured and idealistic lass who wrote poetry and joined service clubs and helped her mother care for her two younger brothers. Named after Joan of Arc, she had her namesake's stoic selflessness and dedication to the greater good, despite personal hardship.

She met the wild young man she would marry on a blind date while in college. Ed Farrell was everything her father disapproved of in a suitor for his only daughter, rebellious, freethinking, politically radical and Irish. Not to mention, whimsical. Their courtship was interrupted by World War Two into which Ed was drafted as an infantry private after having turned down an officer's commission.

He served with the 136th Antiaircraft Battalion as a noncommissioned officer, landing on the beaches of Normandy on D-day plus three, and spent his war shooting down German buzz bombs near Antwerp and lying about in mud-filled trenches writing poetry for my mother as well as undertaking a 700-mile escapade returning in a jeep through parts of France not 100% cleared of enemy troops to retrieve the battalion commander's toilet seat which had been left behind on Omaha Beach, all the while lugging his footlocker filled with books by F. Scott Fitzgerald, James Joyce and Ernest Hemingway.

The pairing of the German good girl and the Irish rebel resulted in a twenty-seven year marriage and a friendship that survived divorce and endured until my father's death. It resulted also in the creation of a family through birth and adoption that united people of five races:

white, black, Hispanic, Native American and Oriental. Seven children around the table, a round table like that of Arthur's knights, seven young faces of different skin tones and features looked to Ed and Jody Farrell for guidance and encouragement, life and love.

As a child I adored and feared my father. When he was away, I missed him. Upon his return, it seemed the house turned topsy-turvy, his energy, disruptiveness and his drinking upsetting a delicate balance my mother struggled to maintain. With so many kids and our respective friends and followers in and out, the house at 152 Buena Vista was like Grand Central Station of the West. It was the sixties and seventies and the hippy movement was in full flower. Our living-room floor was a favored stopping place for young people moving up and down the California coast, "looking for America." The hippy movement tickled my father's rebellious streak and he added to the hub-bub by bringing home lost wayfarers he found in his travels: Flower children and rainbow-chasers; drug addicts and drunken tramps; even foreign sailors he brought home for Thanksgiving dinner from the San Francisco docks.

Jody, in her good nature, put up with this, stretching our meals to meet the requirements of more hungry mouths, finding floor space and blankets to bed down the indigent, mothering the motherless and befriending the friendless.

It seems in looking back, that my father stirred things up and my mother settled things down. My father was like the storm, whose lightning strikes crashed from wall to wall in Tokopah Canyon in Sequoia National Park, roaring, flashing and booming, sending a chill up the spine and a tingle in the flesh, deluging the mountain with drenching rain and stinging hail. My mother was like the Marble Fork of the Kaweah River that ran without surcease from the high Tablelands to the San Joaquin Valley floor, picking up all the run-off, calming the flood, gathering all the waterways into one stream, and flowing pure and sweet, fresh with bubbling white water in the narrow passes and widening to sparkling clarity in the sandy boulder-strewn flats, bringing the water, the fresh, pure, life-giving water to the broad green valley to nurture the meadows, to draw a sprout from the sleeping seed.

Despite their different natures, my parents were united in their belief in the goodness of humanity, their compassion for all living creatures, their love of music and the arts, and their dedication to righting the wrongs of history.   Their first adoption, that of my older brother Andy, was of a neglected and possibly abused 18-month-old who had been placed several times unsuccessfully. The adoption agency people feared for the little boy's life if he didn't soon find a family to bond with and stay with. A little red truck rolled playfully between my dad, my mom and my oldest sister, Susan, convinced the little boy that perhaps this was the family for him. He was right, it was the family for him. He came home the following day. And never looked back.

Here was a big jolly man for a father, a gentle patient woman for a mother, and two older sisters (Susan and Elly) and a brother (Steve) to play with, but it was my mother who held and cuddled the little boy who at first was largely unresponsive to her affections. It was my mother who rocked the cradle, crooned the lullabies, lovingly bathed and dressed, fed and loved, kissed and snuggled the little boy. It was she who worked with him so diligently on the schoolwork when he struggled. It was she who ran to his bedside when the night fears came for him. It was she who let him know how deeply he was loved when his wounded heart tried to close against the pain which comes of loving. She who took a solitary and uncertain soul and built him into the solid structure of a family. She did this for all of us. To greater or lesser degrees, we each of us had our special needs. Each child is one of a kind, we bring with us our own inner terrors and our own triumphs. Whether this is the result of past lives or something else, I don't know, but my mother was there for each of them, for all of us.

The interracial adoptions were an answer to the injustice of past racism, a demonstration of my parent's belief that there is only one race, that being the human one. There had been a story in the news of a white minister and his wife who had adopted a black child only to return it to the agency after their congregation protested their adoption of the child. My parents actually contacted the agency offering to adopt the child but were told it had already been placed. There were, however, other children of various racial backgrounds who needed placement, they were told. We Farrells were taught there is one family, the family of Man. Our own family illustrated it.

Ed and Jody believed that it is with one small action at a time that the world is made a better place, one child at a time that the world is saved. The little things are where we make a difference. Just as it is the little things from which the construction worker builds the world. It is the nuts and bolts, the nails and boards, the rocks and the trees. I learned from my parents how to aspire and fail, how to struggle and succeed. When we fail it is not due to outside influences but rather to our own sabotage. When we succeed, it is because we attend to the little things while keeping mindful of the big picture. I am my parents' daughter: For me success is not measured in monetary rewards nor in celebrity fortune and fame, but in the measure of what I have come to mean to the people around me, those with whom I share the air.

Did I do good work? Put in an honest day for an honest wage?

Yes, I was proud that I did that every day, no matter the obstacles.

Did I ease the way for anyone? Did I make a connection?

Whenever I could, I would help a co-worker, try to connect as a fellow human being, no matter how badly they may have treated me. I never held a grudge but always gave each person the respect of expecting good behavior out of them, despite what their past behavior may have been. I expect the same of myself, and grant myself the same self-respect.

Did I save a life? Maybe. Can one ever really know?

Did I bring joy? Sometimes. A smile might crack an otherwise rock-hard face. A hand might clap me upon the shoulder.

Did I seek the truth? Always. The truth never frightened me.

Did I stand up for what was right? Always, no matter what it might cost. Did I lend someone else the strength to do the same?

Perhaps by example.

Like my mother and father.

30

A Lasting Contribution
In which my mother makes a creative living

Memories of my childhood are memories of colors and of smells. Memories of sounds and senses, and of touches.

I remember striped curtains of umber, burgundy and beige framing windows looking out upon a green and overgrown garden, where robins got drunk on berries and butterflies landed on my hand. I remember my mother's hands and apron white with flour, the smell of baking bread and the sight of butter warming in a dish. I remember tissue paper patterns laid out on the table pinned to fabric bought at J.C. Penney's, my mother with more pins in her mouth, cutting the cloth with a large pair of metal scissors, clunk! clunk! clunk! and the whirring of the Singer sewing machine as she made our clothing. I remember apples baking in the oven, stuffed with walnuts, dates and cinnamon for a sweet dessert.

I remember my mother's hands in my hair as she tried to comb the blackberry twigs and the windblown tangles from it, her voice in my ear as she said, "You're a wild little Indian, aren't you?" I remember a golden retriever with a tennis ball in his mouth following me into the house with his paws dark with mud from the creek, my mother's admonishment to the two of us, "Ack, Amy, take Jason outside and wash his feet. Yours too."

I remember my mother wiping the vinyl disc with a paper towel, blowing on it, setting the needle and letting the dulcet notes of Joan Baez flow from the stereo speakers, "...farewell, Angelina..." I remember Donovan, "...try and catch the wind." Joni Mitchell, "...you don't know what you've got 'til its gone." Simon and Garfunkel, "...words of the prophets are written on the subway walls." Cat Stevens singing about a moon shadow, "Leaping and dancing..."

I remember my mother in blue jeans on hands and knees weeding a garden patch to grow vegetables for our table and planting impatiens and Cala Lilly bulbs for the beauty of them. I remember her holding a gray cat whose eyes seemed as large, lovely and wise as her own. I remember listening to my mother and father arguing, my ear pressed to a door and Elly at my elbow whispering, "What are they saying?" Remember hearing the tears, the hurt and anger in my mother's trembling voice as she said, "Eddy, why are you doing this to us?" And I remember the warm safe embrace of her arms as she held us children through the storm that had become her life.

Jody had ridden the wild ride of Ed's stormy ways and she had smoothed the path for his children, making it possible for us to love him. And for many years, making it possible for him to come and go at will, igniting and disrupting our lives even as she soothed and harmonized them. Finally, however, she had deemed it necessary to cut free the bobbing boat that threatened to drag the family down with it, to let drift wherever it was bound, or to founder if it would.

I never begrudged my valiant mother anything she needed to do for her self-preservation, I know at what cost to her own soul she made the sacrifices she did each day to keep our family safe and secure, to try to give us the childhood all children should have, despite whatever storms raged about us. In fact, I would, years later, follow in her steps and make a similar decision in circumstances as dire.

Her husband gone from the house, four kids still under her roof, the bills mounting and little or no money coming in, my mother was in a desperate state. It was 1972 and she had not held a job outside the home since her marriage twenty-seven years before. Now she carried the full responsibility for feeding and sheltering her brood. The garage my father had once renovated into a studio my mother now rented out as a living space with kitchen and bathroom rights. She rented the master bedroom to a young couple and moved into the tiny upstairs bedroom which Elly had vacated upon moving to an Oregon tree farm with her boyfriend, David. Another bedroom was also rented out. We got on food stamps and with the boarders leading the charge, went on dumpster-diving forays behind the Safeway store to augment our larder. Somehow, we squeaked by. But my mother still needed a paying job.

Having participated in a workshop run by Dr. Maria Rickers, a Russian émigré and a foremost authority on the Rorschach method of psychoanalysis, my mother had recently begun volunteering at Napa State hospital working with the mentally ill. Necessity being the mother of invention, she now took this work to a higher level, solicited funding from the County Mental Health Agency and opened a "creative living center" in our home.

The five-bedroom family home in Mill Valley was outfitted for therapy group sessions and for art, creative writing, music and movement therapy. In addition, the clients (who attended on an outpatient basis), spent time each week in grocery shopping, meals preparation and cleaning up after themselves. They took field trips to public parks, libraries and museums using public transportation, and in a variety of other ways learned how to function in the world outside hospitals and institutions. They were guided by staff members hired and trained by my mother, and by interns and volunteers, all overseen by County Mental Health.

My mother found a need and filled it. She needed a way to support herself and her children. There was a body of mental health patients needing to transition from being institutionalized to being self-sufficient. Funding had been cut from the budgets of many standard institutions and patients were being released from hospitals. The

Creative Living Center (CLC) gave them a place to go, taught them how to recapture their own lives and gave them the knowledge they needed to manage their time, showing them how to shop and cook and take care of themselves, in a supportive environment, all the while continuing treatment of the mental conditions which had landed them in institutions in the first place. The exposure to art, creative writing, music, dance, yoga and movement was not only a method to continue psychoanalysis but a way to enhance their appreciation of life and all that makes it sweet.

It was a new concept in therapy and it worked. It worked not only in terms of the benefits to the clients but in the way it was a "creative living" for my mother in supporting her many children in the absence of a bread-winning father.

Because of its success, the Creative Living Center grew, like an edifice built stone upon stone. Soon, with the help of grant monies, CLC was able to buy two houses in San Rafael, California and expand its services. My mother was the director of CLC for eighteen years until her retirement in 1990. My mother built something of an idea and of her heart and soul.

I was building things of nails and boards, wet cement and hammered rocks.

31

Whimsy

In which I get an unexpected body-piercing

A sixteen-penny duplex (double-headed forming nail) is a pretty hefty little piece of steel, about three inches long and an eighth-inch in diameter. A pretty nasty little spear, especially when it's headed right for one's unprotected face at about 60 miles an hour.

I was working in Sequoia Park at the new Wuksachi Village firehouse construction project. A guy named Brice and I were told to go strip forms off of some concrete columns that had been poured the previous week. These columns would later be veneered in mortared stone. I grabbed my three foot crowbar from the back of my truck and walked over there. The forms on the columns were affixed to the slab floor by 2x4 boards that had holes drilled through and thence drilled into the concrete floor. Two big duplex nails were then hammered side by side through the wood and into the floor. They were driven as far as the first head to secure the form wood and then could be pulled by hooking a claw hammer or crowbar to the second head and prying it up.

Brice and I were working separate columns, prying nails out and then freeing the plywood forms, chucking the wood into a big pile.

I liked Brice, he was a hard worker and had always treated me respectfully. He was about my height, with red hair and beard and snapping green eyes. We had ended up on several jobs together over the years and Brice had never once joined in on the hazing and harassment I had so often gotten from the other men. He had also never come to my defense, but you can't have everything. Maybe unlike my parents, his had never taught him that if you're not part of the solution, you're part of the problem. But I give him a pass simply because it was nice to work with someone and just work with someone, not work with someone and always have to be on guard.

We were chatting about old trucks while we worked. Brice owned a 1956 Chevrolet Apache and I was telling him about a 1957 GMC I had once owned. "It had a Hydromatic transmission," I said. "You know what that is?"

I hooked my crowbar on one nail and pressed down on the bar. The nail would not slide out.

"Sure," Brice answered, "like an early automatic."

"Exactly," I said, throwing my weight on the bar again. The nail wouldn't budge. "Only you shifted just like a manual. H-pattern on the column." I repositioned my feet and laid into it with everything I had. Bing! The nail flew out of the form as if shot from a gun. Thwack! I felt something hit me in the lower lip. I looked down and saw the big nail bobbing in front of my chin. Too cool, I thought.

"Only there was no clutch to push in," Brice was saying.

"Hey, Brithe!" I lisped "Check thith thout!" I walked over to Brice's column and tapped his shoulder. This was so weird, I just had to show someone! He spun around and his eyes bugged out. "Ohhh, that's gross!" he shouted, taking a step back. The sixteen-penny duplex nail was sticking out of my lower lip. It had struck with enough force to go clean through the flesh and lodge its tip between my front two bottom teeth, just at the gum line. Surprisingly, it didn't really hurt much!

"Watch thith," I lisped. I wiggled my jaw back and forth, which, because the tip of the nail was lodged between my front teeth, made the nail swing left then right then left again. I chuckled, then made the nail go up and down, up and down. This was funny!

"Oh, man!" Brice cried, "I'm gonna puke!"

I thought about leaving the nail in and seeing how long it would stay before it fell out on its own. It was a little bit of construction-site whimsy, like the Haight-Ashbury whimsy of my dad wearing the Fedora until the wrapping paper fell off of its own accord. Bobbing the nail up and down and swinging it back and forth a few more times, I gauged my co-worker's reaction and thought better of it. If Brice up-chucked, he might go home sick for which he'd get shit-canned. Worse, I would have to do all the work myself. And lose my only friend on this job. With a resigned sigh, I reached up, grasped the nail and jerked it out of my lip. A trickle of blood ran down my chin and all the way into the neck of my T-shirt. My lip felt a little numb and the puncture stung just a little bit once the air hit it.

"That's sick!" Brice said. I laughed and went back to pulling nails, leaving the ribbon of blood on my chin like a red badge of courage. "Just watch out," I said, "it could happen to you too."

"Amy, you're one tough cookie," Brice said. "I've worked with some guys that'd pass out when shit like that happened to them."

"I don't pass out easy," I said,

Brice said, "No shit. But you're lucky that nail didn't go into your eye! You might have passed out then."

I stopped pulling nails and stared at him, holding my crowbar. He looked at me with the blood running down my chin. "I take it back," he said. "You'd probably keep on working with the thing in your eyeball."

I laughed. "We <u>should</u> probably be wearing goggles," I said.

Later, when Brice told the rest of the crew about me and the nail, they didn't believe him. The next day and for the following week, I had a purple bruise the size of a quarter below my lower lip, with a tiny red scab at the center of it. **Now, that hurt like hell!**

32

Flagging Expectations
In which I finally end up a flagger
(at least for a little while)

The radio on my hip crackled.

"Okaayyy," drawled Crysstal at the flag station at the other end of the project, "the last cah has two ruhlly cute guys in it, oveh."

I pulled the device off my belt, held it to my mouth and keyed the mike. "Crysstal," I said, "What color and make is the last car, over?"

Crackle. "Oohh, Ah don't know, muhbe green or gray, but them two fellahs, one has a totally awesome little blond mustache, sooo cute, oveh!"

I sighed. Ever since the other flag-girl had gone home from the job pregnant, I had had to fill in. Tough as I was, and able to do any job on a construction site, there were times I had to flag traffic. It had been a week of this now and I was weary of it. "Crysstal!" I barked into the radio, "you have got to tell me the color and type of the last car you send through. If you don't know the make, at least tell me what color it is and whether it's a two-door sedan, a four-door, a pickup truck or whatever! Over!"

Crackle. "Whatevah!"

The line of cars was visible now, snaking its way towards me, raising a cloud of dust as it approached. This was another job in the High Sierra, the repair and widening of part of a popular highway to mountain recreation areas. The crew had one lane completely torn up and the other lane had to serve both traffic and the equipment to perform the work, consequently Crysstal and I had to stop both directions of traffic for 20 minute periods to let the crew and machinery work, then the crew would move to the side and we'd have 20 minutes to let traffic go through, one direction at a time. This made for slow production, a testy job super, and an even testier public. Now I was getting testy because my coworker was a Valley Girl Ditz!

As the cars streamed past me, cloaking me in dust, I was actually praying for a water truck driver with a malicious streak to come by and douse me. At least it would settle this dust. I waited for what looked like the last car, scanning the occupants to see if they were two really cute guys, one of whom had a totally awesome little blond mustache, but the dust swirling around me made it hard to see inside the vehicle. It passed and through the dust haze came yet more vehicles. I leaned on my tall Stop/Slow paddle and waited.

One of the cars in my lineup honked its horn. I gave them a friendly smile and a "just wait a little bit more" universal hand gesture, but the fever was on them now and pretty soon every driver was leaning on their horn. Finally, amid the din, I squinted down the road and saw what looked like Crysstal's last car, a green Toyota Tercel with two young male occupants. As it whizzed by, the awesomely mustachioed driver grinned like a Cheshire cat as he turned his wheel abruptly and showered me with dirt and gravel. "Shit! Godammit!" I shouted as I jumped aside and tried to shield my face from his rooster tail of flying debris. "Asshole!" I shouted after him.

Recovering my composure, I returned to my previous position, only to find that the first car in my lineup was edging its way around my barrier of orange traffic cones, trying to go around and enter the lane. I waved my Stop paddle aggressively at him and stood in his way until I got him stopped. Then I turned to see if the way was still clear to send my line through. I heard the roar of the big Cat front loader starting up and the machine's back-up bell started clanging as it moved backwards into the lane and began working. Shit! Twenty minutes was up and I hadn't been able to send my cars through!

The other machines were now busily pushing boulders and tree stumps around and the front loader was dumping loads of dirt in the lane. The laborers and other tradesmen were swarming all over with shovels and other tools, happily working at their accustomed duties. At my back the driver of the errant car honked angrily and his cohorts in the other vehicles soon took up the hue and cry again. I looked wistfully at the job. Oh happy laborers! I thought, oh wretched me!

On union construction jobs, the task of traffic control (or "flagging") falls to the laborer. Any laborer on the job may get assigned this duty or if there are union flag-women on the board down at the union hall, they would be brought on. In Local 294, there were around five or six females who were in the union solely for the flagging jobs. At the time, I was the only female in the local who considered herself a laborer first and would prefer to pick up a muck-stick or do any other job like the male laborers did.

Anyone who thinks flagging traffic is easy money should try it for a day. They would soon eat their words. Besides being one of the most dangerous of jobs in construction, it is stressful, exhausting, uncomfortable (subject to all weather conditions and temperatures and being a victim of your own unrelieved bladder most of the time!), backbreaking (try standing in place on hard pavement all day), by turns exceeding tedious and way-too-exciting (like when trying to dodge a speeding vehicle that fails to respond to the advance warning signs and then locks up its brakes and begins swerving just before it reaches you) and more likely to involve you in a bout of roadside fisticuffs (with disgruntled motorists) than any other job.

I turned back to my charges and approached the first car. Signaling for the driver to roll down the window, I said as politely as I could, "Sir, you'll have to back your car back into the line."

"How come you didn't let us go through?" he demanded petulantly.

"I'm very sorry, sir, but we ran out of time. We only are allowed 20 minutes to clear traffic before the work has to begin again."

"Well, damn it, you need to take turns then!"

"Yes, sir, you will be the next to go," I informed him.

"How long will that be?"

"Twenty minutes from now."

"God damn it all!" the man exploded. "You know how long I've already been waiting here?"

These sentiments were expressed by several other drivers, many of whom stepped out of their cars to surround me and complain, vehemently. As soon as I could sweet-talk them all back into their cars, I stepped back to my line of traffic cones and radioed my fellow flagger. "Crysstal, next time I get to send my cars through first."

Crackle. "Uuuv course," she drawled. "Donchuu think Ah know that?"

"Yeah, well, you sent through so many cars I never got a chance to send any of mine and now they're all mad as hell."

Crackle. "Way-ell, Ah did have a slew of 'em ovah he-yah."

"I know, I have a slew of them here too. But we can't send all of them through at one time. I'll send half of mine and then you send half of yours and that way the ones that have waited the longest get to go through. The later arrivals will just have to wait their turn."

Crackle. "Way-ell, Ah'll try but folks don't like you stopping 'em when you've just sent through the folks ahead of 'em."

"Cry me a river," I said.

Crackle. "Way-ell, they might turn violent. Ah don't feel like gettin' muh face rearranged. It's hard on the make-up!"

Crackle.

33

Out Of Control
In which I find you can't really control traffic

I laughed despite myself. That girl applied her makeup with a mason's trowel.

Rearranging her face through all the spackle might prove difficult even for the most violent of motorists. She was right about the tempers of the driving public though. Several times I have been almost run over by accident and on purpose while flagging. I have been slapped on the ass by a passenger in an errant car so hard (due to the rate of speed) that it threw me onto my hands and knees. I have been pointedly threatened with violence and verbally abused.

On occasions when I have asked my bosses why I am being selected of all the laborers on the crew to flag the traffic, I have invariably been told, "Women make better flaggers. They have more of a calming effect on the public, because they know how to talk people down. They are less likely to get in fist fights with trouble-making drivers." Perhaps if I hauled off and slugged more motorists, I mused, I wouldn't have to flag traffic ever again.

The sound of car doors slamming woke me out of my flagging reverie. Maybe more disgruntled motorists were heading my way. I glanced back at my line of vehicles which had grown so long I could no longer see the end of it where it disappeared around the next bend in the mountain road. Families were exiting their vehicles, opening their trunks and camper shells and getting out picnic supplies. Kids were playing in the roadway and slipping off the pavement to skip about in the forest. I heaved a sigh of relief. If they were playing Robin Hood, they would not be whining at their parents and inciting them to violence. If the moms and dads were spreading mayo on white bread with pre-sliced cheese and pastrami, they would be too busy to contemplate mayhem.

Soon the chatter and laughter of children playing came to my ears through the woods. Clack! Clack! Clack! I walked to the road shoulder where I could get a better view of their game. They were indeed playing Robin of Sherwood. About twelve kids were dashing about amongst the pines sword-fighting ...with survey stakes!

I left my Stop paddle upright in a tall traffic cone and ran into the forest. The kids had striped the whole area of all the survey stakes which a survey crew had spent three days setting for the next phase of the road widening project. As I looked, I saw that the twelve kids I had seen were only the beginning. All down the line, kids from the waiting cars had decided the Sherwood forest game was a good one. In fact, some of the little terrors had piles of survey stakes and were industriously sticking them into the soft forest duff, making little forts to hide in.

Oh my God! I thought, the Super is gonna kill me! But before I even had time to yell at the kids, the air horn blew up on the project and it was my turn to send the cars through. "Leave those sticks right there," I hollered and pointed to the cars, "it's time to go!"

The children shrieked, dropped their swords (most of them) and ran for their respective vehicles. "Sending mine through, over!" I barked into my radio, turning my Stop paddle to Slow and waving the first car into the open lane. As the long line passed me, covering me in a cloud of dust, I keyed my mike again. "Crysstal, do you copy?" Crackle. Crackle.

"Crysstal, I repeat, do you read me?" Crackle. Crackle.

"Shit!" The radio batteries must be going dead. Our flagging stations were about a mile apart and the terrain was up and down. Only a very high quality set of walkie-talkies were reliable and the batteries had to be fully charged. In event of loss of radio com, there was only one way to communicate, the old fashioned way.

I picked up an orange traffic flag. Knowing I had to select one vehicle to be the last car, I tried to find a gap in the line as the traffic streamed by. They had been waiting so long and there were so many that there was no gap. Oh well, I would have to create one. I turned my paddle from Slow to Stop and waved it at a pickup truck. The driver, a big burly fellow, acted like he would not stop, so I stepped aggressively out into the lane, waving my paddle. Uttering a curse, the man braked. "Ah, just let me go through!" he complained. "I been waiting 45 minutes!"

"Well, I am going to let you go through as a matter of fact," I said, "but you have to do me a favor." I handed him the orange flag. "You're the last vehicle I'm letting through, so I need you to give this flag to the flagger on the other end."

"Sure," the man said, reaching for the flag.

"It's really important that you remember, because if she doesn't get the flag, she won't know it's clear. She'll wait and wait."

"Why don't you use radios?" The man said, as he put his truck in gear and pulled away. The vehicle behind him tried to blast past me but I stepped in front of it, glaring at the driver and waving my Stop in his face. He skidded to a halt almost hitting me. "Why'd you let him go and not me?!" the driver yelled.

"I'm very sorry, but you have to take turns," I said.

"I've been waiting as long as him," he protested.

"Again, I'm sorry. Each side only gets about ten minutes to send traffic through." I looked at my line of cars, stretching around the bend out of sight. The horns were beginning to honk again. I hoped that the queue didn't extend back beyond the construction signing which warned drivers in advance of possible stopped traffic ahead. If such were the case, with these winding roads, if drivers came around a corner and traffic was stopped in front of them, there could be a serious collision. But I didn't have time to worry about that now.

My primary concern was whether Crysstal had indeed waited to send her traffic through knowing it was my turn. If she wanted to be a bitch and sent hers through and then I sent mine through as well, we would have a situation where fifty cars would be trying to go one way and fifty would be trying to go the other way and they would meet in the middle in the single lane. If there wasn't an accident to make matters worse, just getting the opposing traffic cleared out of the work zone would still be a hell of a trick!

I was also worried that the pickup driver might not give Crysstal the flag or that she might not give the flag to her last driver, or if she did, she wouldn't explain the procedure to them and they wouldn't give it to me but drive past me with it sitting on the floorboards, forgotten.. I would wait and wait, not knowing if the last car was really truly the last. The work would begin and go on for the prescribed twenty minutes and when the equipment cleared off the lane, I would have to send my traffic through with no flag to give them and no way to communicate. This whole flagging operation would very quickly become one great big huge FUBAR (fucked up beyond all recognition)!

Perhaps I was overanalyzing. Perhaps I was a worrywart. Perhaps I was stressing out for no good reason. But experience had taught me that in flagging, Murphy's Law was the only law. Unlike Crysstal, who was new at the game, I had, on other jobs, been a flagger months at a time where the only system we had was the old-fashioned one. No radios, just passing the flag hour after hour, day by day, week after week.

Hundreds of drivers were stopped, handed the flag and told to deliver it to the flagger at the other end. Most were capable of such an easy task, some were forgetful and drove right on through without passing off the flag, causing delays for their fellow travelers and confusion in the workings of the job. Some were outright mischievous and would mess with us by dropping the flag over the side of the road as soon as they were out of our sight or simply keeping it as a trophy, laughing all the way home. These jobs were frustrating and stressful.

I was glad when radio usage became the norm on construction jobs and the passing of the flag went the way of the dodo.

34

It Takes A Flagger
In which one gets by me

A lot of things can go wrong on a flagging operation and when they go wrong, people get hurt. Flagging is an interactive activity, requiring a person who is strong of character, forceful, communicative and assertive. This person has to have an active mind, be capable of anticipating problems and making sound, often split-second, decisions to avert disaster.

It is not a job for introverts or wall-flowers. An extroverted personality who can approach strangers and tell them in clear concise language what is going on and how they are expected to behave and/or can use broad, simple and clear body language to convey directions, such a person makes the best flagger.

A self-contained person who can work alone yet is comfortable dealing with the public, has a positive attitude and doesn't get easily bored, can stay focused and motivated, such a person can excel at flagging traffic.

It helps if you have the protective nature of a grizzly bear mother, as well. If you care deeply about the safety of your coworkers and of the population at large, then you will naturally exert the influence over the motorists that is needed to keep everyone safe as the traffic passes through the work zone.

Alertness is critical, especially in complex flagging operations, such as long stretches of roadway with multiple intersections and a moving repair operation such as chip-sealing where a pilot car is being used. Each flagger, positioned at the various intersections, must be aware at all times of the position and direction of travel of the pilot car with its following of vehicles. On a long day with a constantly changing tactical situation, it is easy to zone out and forget which way traffic is moving, and in which direction lies the work crew, since the crew and equipment is traveling up and down the roadway, moving from one end to the other of the work zone.

There must be a reliable radio com system so that each flagger knows exactly what is going on minute to minute. Traffic which wants to go in one direction may be allowed to go through, while traffic going in another direction must be held until the pilot car is going that way. Each driver must be interviewed to learn where they are headed and then told whether they can go or must wait. This work is highly interactive and very exacting. One mistake can cause a traffic collision or an injury to a worker, or at least cause havoc on the project or result in tort claims against the company.

Flagging traffic is a skilled labor job and is definitely not "easy money." Those folks work for a living and have a great load of responsibility on their shoulders.

Once, when I was flagging for a blasting operation, the federal job inspector got so used to just waving at me and driving around my flagging station to go inspect the job, that he did the same thing on the day of the big blast. I had let him get away with it on so many previous occasions that I had no control over him when it was critical that I should have.

So here he came on blast day, zipping past me into the danger zone! What he didn't know and I did, was that just before he came whipping by in his white Suburban, the 30 second air horn had gone off. I was waving frantically at him with my Stop paddle as he steered quickly around me but he didn't even notice! As he disappeared from my sight into the blast zone, I felt the tremor of the very earth under my feet and heard the Ka-boom! Ka-Boom! Ka-Boom! Ka-Boom! of the shot.

I was standing there, numb with shock, picturing the inspector reduced to a bloody unrecognizable mass inside an overturned and smoking wreck of Detroit steel, when a voice behind me said, "Did that guy just get blown up?" It was a driver who had gotten out of his car and was standing near me.

I gulped hard.

"Yeah, yeah, I think so. I mean, I hope not."

Amy R Farrell

35

The Donager
In which I narrowly avoid another big rock

That inspector never lived it down, but he did live.

Like a guy with a death wish, or maybe like a Hollywood stunt driver with a death wish, the whole blasting crew witnessed him careening right by the set charges, the big white Suburban passing each charge just before it blew.

The blasted granite rose up gently and dropped smoothly back into place as he drove by, as if his passage caused the land itself to snap like a housewife shaking out a blanket. He pulled up next to the crew and parked the vehicle, climbed out and looked at them hiding behind a large boulder.

"What was that noise? Did I miss something?" he asked. "Why are you guys hiding?"

The flagger stands between the public and death.

I once flagged traffic on a mountain job where a John Deere 790 excavator was in the roadway, scooping up big round granite boulders from the uphill side of the road and swinging them over the road to drop them off on the downhill side. My flag station was only about 60 feet away and I was watching the operator perform this highly skilled maneuver as I held traffic up, marveling that he could do it without a "thumb" on his excavator bucket.

He would just scoop the boulder and jiggle the bucket until he got the teeth under the rock then he would lift and jiggle until the rock slid onto the bucket. The rock being too big to fit inside the bucket, the operator would curl the bucket back towards the arm until the rock was pinned between the teeth and the arm. Then he would rotate the machine so that he could drop the rock off the down side. The big rocks would roll down the mountain, crashing and smashing into pine trees until they finally came to rest somewhere far below.

As I was enjoying the entertainment of watching this skilled union equipment operator play with boulders and his huge powerful machine, an impatient driver edged his car around my traffic cones without my notice. Before I could stop him, he gunned his little Honda Civic past me and was gleefully escaping my trap.

"Stop!" I squawked and started running after him. I could see the faces of his children looking at me from their car seats as I ran alongside the car, see his wife turn and make eye contact with me and then say something admonishing to her husband.

The car suddenly skidded to a halt and I stopped beside it, panting. The roar of the 790 was loud in my ears and I felt the hot breath of the machine blasting my body. I looked up and saw that the car and I were below the suspended arm of the excavator. The machine was in mid-swing, the arm extended out so that the rock would fall well off the road, the rock pinched against the arm. When the operator saw the car he reacted instinctively, stopping the machine. He would have done better to keep it moving.

The sudden stop caused the huge "donager" pinched between the teeth and the arm to shake loose. As I watched, petrified, the rock above me begin to slide off the bucket of the excavator. Its trajectory was the little Civic full of family and the flagger, me, standing beside it. The grind of the granite boulder over the steel of the bucket was earsplitting. For an instant, I caught the eye of the operator where he sat, safe in the enclosed cab high above me, his hands poised on the joystick controls.

His eyes were as wide as mine.

Luckily, he was one of those "golden" operators who could do just about anything with just about any machine. His big hands, blue-veined and callused, rough and gnarled from years of construction work, moved in barely perceptible motions, like the wings of a dragonfly as it dips and dives over a pond.

The boulder, about two-thirds the size of the car, slid slowly towards the teeth of the machine and the open air above my head. The tiny delicate motions of the hands on the levers transmitted, through some miracle of the science of hydraulics, a series of commands to the lifeless steel of the big machine, and it proceeded to save my life and the lives of the hapless family in the Honda.

The machine's arm dropped down, towards me, and the bucket curled outward, away from me, opening like a flower. The rock, whose great weight could only follow the pull of gravity, shifted and rolled backward away from the teeth and towards the hinge of the bucket. Once it crashed against the back of the bucket, the bucket changed direction, curling inward again, locking the rock against the arm. These three maneuvers were done so quickly, so smoothly, that it all happened in a matter of seconds and the rock which would have crushed us was once again held firmly by the machine, and the operator toed his machine back into its pivot, bringing the rock and its danger away over our heads and to the far side of the road.

When he released the rock, it rolled and crashed down the mountainside, shivering full grown pine trees and making a terrible racket until it silenced itself against its fellows with a final great Crack! in the canyon below.

We all breathed a great simultaneous sigh of relief!

And the little Civic and its occupants drove on.

36

Dead On Arrival

In which another gets by me

You come to expect a little danger when you flag traffic
for any length of time, because if it hasn't happened to you, you've heard
the tales of flaggers being smeared by semis or crushed up against guard
rails by errant vehicles.

On one job I had flagging traffic for a bridge repair on the main
highway into Yosemite National Park, my flag station was on a downhill
grade that wound down through thick forest on both sides. No matter
how many advance warning signs we put out on that grade, people still
would not slow down. They would come barreling around the curve,
see me and my cones and Stop paddle and lock up their brakes.

By the time they got their vehicle stopped they'd be a hundred
feet past me. Some would touch their brakes as they flew on by me,
then figure "Oh well, too late now," and just keep on going. After a few
near misses on my coworkers on the bridge, I decided that even if it
meant standing in the traffic lane until the last moment, it was better to

risk myself than see three or four men killed. At least I had my eye on the traffic and could jump aside, the laborers on the crew were busy and would be sitting ducks. So I'd stand there in the lane, waving my Stop at the cars, then at the very last minute, I'd jump clear as they went streaking by, brakes squealing, finally coming to a halt in a blue cloud of their own burnt tire rubber.

Risky, yeah, but I admit, it was a little fun!

As the job progressed, the job boss added more and more bright orange Road Work Ahead and Flagman Ahead and Prepare To Stop signs on that downhill grade, but nothing helped. Each morning, I took an armload of cones around the bend from my station and laid them out for about a hundred feet before the bend as a way of alerting the drivers that the road project was right around that corner but the drivers acted as if all the neon orange cones were just more pine trees.

The worst driver of all was the lady who drove the school bus up from Oakhurst into Yosemite and back, taking the Park employee's kids to school. My fellow flagger, Fritz, at the bottom end of the project dubbed her, "Lock 'em up Sally," because of the way she'd blast past me and then smoke her brakes all the way through the job site, causing workers to scatter like chickens in those old spaghetti Westerns when the bad guys ride into town. It was amazing that she kept her job, especially with all those kids on board. You'd think at least one kid would get home and tell mommy or daddy about the crazy reckless school bus lady. If she drove like that through a construction zone, you know she was equally nuttsy on the treacherous mountain route to Yosemite and back. That old International bus was no Lamborghini, after all!

On a chip-seal job on State Highway 190, I had a flagging station set up with all the usual advance signing plus a huge message board that Caltrans had provided. This one driver somehow missed all that and flew past me at upwards of 70 miles an hour. I was waving my Stop paddle frantically at him as he streamed past because somewhere up ahead and I wasn't sure exactly where, was an oiler rig and a chip-spreader and a roller and a broom-truck and a whole bunch of transfer-trailer trucks and a lot of workers I didn't want to see get killed.

Well, this guy sees me as he speeds by, a split second of eye contact, and he locks up his brakes, turning his steering wheel ever so slightly to the right. At that rate of speed even a slight change of direction was too much. His car turned sideways, skidded a hundred feet or so, flipped over and then proceeded to flip, flip, flip, flip, flip until it left the highway, took out the cyclone highway fence, crossed the frontage road and ended up (upside-down) in the front yard of a house about 1500 feet down the highway, in a cloud of dust and settling debris.

For the following two hours, I observed from my flagging station, the police and emergency personnel arrive, buzzing like bees around the scene of the accident, extracting the man from the twisted wreckage, interviewing witnesses, removing the hulk of the car from the front yard, dragging the remnants of the cyclone fence out of the frontage road and piling it on the highway shoulder. I expected an officer would come interview me for his report but none ever came over. Later, my foreman came by to inquire whether I needed a rest-room break. I asked him about the man in the car.

"Oh, yeah," my foreman said casually, "DOA." Dead on arrival.

I often travel that section of Highway 190, passing the place where I stood, passing the house where his car sat steaming and smoking in the yard, and think about that last glance, before the man, whoever he was, drove his speeding car right out of this world.

As it turned out, the equipment and workers were a half mile further down the highway, and that he would not have crashed into them if he had just slowed down easily, that if he had pulled over and waited for the pilot car or carefully backed up to where I was, he (whoever he was) would be alive still. He was driving way too fast and distracted, I was waving my Stop aggressively because it was my job to stop cars and control their movements through the job site.

When I see the place where it happened, a lot of questions come up for me. Who was he? Where had he been, where was he going, why was he driving so very fast? Did he often drive like that or was this incident an anomaly? Regardless of the answer, on that day it resulted in his death, the loss to his family (whoever they are) of him and his contributions to their welfare and happiness.

That was over twenty years ago. Sometimes, it seems like yesterday that his eye met mine and then he was gone. It is strange to think that I was the last human contact the man had in this life!

I don't even know his name.

37

Lightning Strikes Twice
In which I begin to feel like a human lightning rod

The weather was looking ominous and I wasn't happy
about it. Nobody loves a good storm more than Yours Truly but not
when I am standing in six inches of water at the bottom of a five foot
trench holding onto an iron pipe which is hanging by a metal chain to
the bucket of a Cat 245 excavator on the exposed flank of a granite
mountainside. The morning on the job had started out in the usual way,
warm and sunny, but shortly after noon the cloud buildup had started
and now the sun was blotted out by heavy dark thunderheads. I could
hear rumbling in the distance. A strong gust of wind or two had caused
my coworkers to glance worriedly skyward and begin talking in fast
Spanish.

Now I was in the trench, holding onto that pipe. The water I
was standing in was the result of showers that had started the previous
day just as work was ending and gone on most of the night. Standing in

water with the sun blazing down on you, your leather work boots soaked through to your socks, was one thing, but standing in water during an electrical storm was another thing entirely! There was a flash of lightning over Siliman Peak, zigzagging against the dark gray sky. I begin to count, one-thousand-one, one thousand-two, one-thousand, then came the thunder. Boom! Boom! BaBoom! The lightning strike was only two and a half miles away.

"Did that scare you, Amy?" the equipment operator we called Tank asked.

I glanced up at him. He liked to be called Tank because his favorite machines to operate were the big ones that had steel track-layers like tanks. He also said he had been a tank-driver in the army. Either explanation was all right by me. He looked like a "Tank," squat, built-solid and iron-faced. He sat there in the enclosed cab of the humming machine, his big hands on the joysticks. The rain begin to patter on my hard hat. I felt large drops slap onto my bare shoulders at the edge of my tank-top. A little while ago I had been sweating in the summer heat. The rain felt cool on my hot skin.

"Anyone who isn't afraid of lightning is a fool," I said.

"Really?" Tank asked. "It doesn't scare me."

That's 'cause you're a fool, I thought. "Lightning kills people," I said. "It's happened right here in this Park. In fact, somebody I knew. Well, kinda knew," I amended.

Tank lowered the pipe and I rammed it home into the bell end of its mate, then shuffled forward and unhooked the chain, letting Tank swing it away for the next pipe. While the men above slung another piece of ductile from the 245's bucket, I stood in the water and looked at the dark sky. There was another flash and another loud series of booms, closer this time. "Shit!" I said aloud, as I scooped up another handful of jelly for the end of the next pipe. The rain was coming a little harder now but not hard enough in itself to shut the job down for the day. It wasn't the rain but the lightning I was concerned about!

Tank pivoted the machine, bringing the 20-ft length of pipe down into the trench. I grabbed hold of it with one hand, steadied it on its suspending chain and smeared the "soap" all over the end of it, then chucked the big rubber glove into the jelly jar and grasped the pipe with two hands. I nodded at Tank and he lowered the load the rest of the way. I rammed it home.

Another flash. More thunder, Boom! Boom! I unhooked the chain and let it slide through my fingers as Tank lifted it clear. "Who did you know that got killed by lightning?" the operator said.

"A surveyor for the National Park," I said. The rain started coming harder now, making little rivulets of mud run down the steep sides of the trench. I took my eyes off the rivulets and looked up at him. "It was 1985. I kinda knew him because I was living at Lodgepole and I knew all the Park people at the time. He was staying in the fire dorm right next to where I lived. He was on the survey crew for this very project in fact," I said, gesturing to my right towards the site selected for the new Wuksachi Village that would in time replace the village in Giant Forest. The trench I was standing in was on the General's Highway just outside the entrance to the Wuksachi site. We were running underground waterline and other utilities for the Village project. I looked back at Tank. "The same day, a bunch of backpackers were struck by lightning on Half Dome in Yosemite. A couple of them died. And people have been killed right here on Moro Rock from being hit by lightning. Aren't you worried about it?" I asked. "I mean, that machine of yours is one big conductor! Solid steel and steel track-layers. It's totally grounded."

He shrugged. "These cabs are insulated," he said. "It's you that'll be fried!"

"Gee thanks!" I said.

Tank laughed. "Fried!" he said. "You know, like fried chick--" he left off the last syllable on purpose. "I always like the succulent breast, myself!"

His little routine was punctuated by another flash of lightning on Siliman Peak, followed by a cymbal-clash of thunder. Before Tank could begin teasing again, one of my other coworkers came over to the edge of the trench and spoke to me, his English heavily accented with Spanish. Jorge had the best English of all the Mexicans on the crew, so he was the designated spokesman. "What, Emmy, you think this storm, it pass soon?"

"I don't know, Jorge," I said. "It doesn't look like it."

Jorge frowned. "Me and the other men, we are thinking that we should be going home now. This storm, it is, how you say, 'crappy weather.'" He gestured to the sky. "It is *peligro*, dangerous," he concluded.

"You're right, Jorge," I said. "Don't worry. Pretty soon the foreman will come and tell us to go home for the day." I wasn't as sure about that as I tried to sound. Jorge looked dubious, but nodded solemnly and walked back to the other men. Another deafening crash of thunder! I looked around hopefully for a white pickup but none was in sight.

Tank smirked at me. He wasn't worried and he was the only regular company man. Jorge and I and the rest of the crew were hired off the board. None of us would walk off the job, we'd be fired for sure so we kept working for another forty-five minutes in the lightning storm, scared to death. The sky was so dark that down at the bottom of the trench, bent over the pipe, I could barely see my own hands as they fumbled with the chain.

"I don't believe this!" someone shouted. I glanced up from unhooking the chain and saw Ken, one of the federal inspectors, standing above me on the lip of the trench. He wore a bright yellow rain slicker and one of those matching fisherman's hats which deflected rainwater off his head and down his back.

"This is bullshit!" he shouted to no one in particular. I was surprised because the entire job I had never heard the man cuss. "Get outta that water, Amy, now!" he ordered.

I slapped the lid on the jelly jar, grasped it by the handle and clambered out of the hole, emerging with heavy mud running down my pants, rainwater dripping from the brim of my hard hat and my boots squish-squishing as I walked over to him.

Ken's dark face turned even darker as he took me in. He was a handsome young black man and had always been very kind and friendly to me. One time he had joined me for lunch where I sat apart from the men reading The Farrier's Journal, and we had engaged in a conversation about being different from the crowd. He had recognized in me someone who could relate to his being the only black engineer in probably a hundred miles. He had told me with deep sadness how his childhood friends from his neighborhood rejected him when he returned home for Christmas holidays, saying he had "sold out" and that he was "trying to be like Whitey." He was a sweet guy and I liked him very much.

"This damned company!" he was raging now. "They know damned well they can't work you people in this kind of weather!"

Another flash arched across the sky.

Then another long series of Boom-boom-boom-rumble-rumble! Ken looked heavenward. The raindrops pelted his face and rivulets of glittering water coursed over his ebony skin. He tipped his head downward and his dark eyes met mine.

"Go! Go, go!" he said. "All of you go! The job is shut down! Come back tomorrow!"

"The boss..." I began.

"I'll be talking with your boss!" Ken said. He turned and glared at Tank. "Shut down that machine! Get the Hell outta this storm before someone gets killed!"

The 245 shut off and Tank picked up his lunch box and began to climb down. Jorge and the Mexicans hadn't had to be told twice, their backs were receding in the distance.

"Thanks, Ken!" I said, as I shoved the jelly jar into the cab of the beat-up old boom truck and slammed the door shut. Lightning flashed and thunder rumbled as I hoofed it to catch up with Jorge and the men who were double-timing-it down the road to where our vehicles were parked.

It was with great relief that I climbed, soaking wet with rain and mud, into my little truck, its rubber tires insulating me from all the electricity flying round in the air, and started down the mountain to Three Rivers. I turned my heater on full-blast, trying to dry my jeans and T-shirt and stop the shivering that had finally set in after getting drenched.

The storm chased me all the way to my home town at the base of the mountains. I got to the Chevron Station in town and pulled in to fill my tank. Standing under the awning protected from the rain, I stomped my feet hard on the concrete, knocking mud out of the tread of my work boots. I was thinking about how I'd have to shed my boots and work clothes on the back patio before stepping into the house naked and heading straight for the shower. Hopefully none of the neighbors would be peering over the backyard fence!

School was getting out just across the street and as I pumped my gas, I watched the children running for mini-vans in the parking lot. Others, whose parents didn't pick them up were holding their heavy book-filled backpacks on their heads as they left the school grounds and began walking home.

Suddenly there was an explosion! KaCRACK!!!

The world went white.

I thought I was dead. I thought the gas pumps had exploded. When I realized I was alive, I found myself on my knees between the gas pump and my Toyota, the nozzle still clutched in my hand. My ears were ringing and my skin tingling strangely.

I stood up and glanced around me. Kids were scattering, moms at mini-vans were staring wide-eyed, people at the gas station were chattering. What was that?

What the hell? God, my ears are ringing! What happened?

I looked at the thin thread of vapor rising from the steel post across the street, the one that holds a chain across the parking lot entrance when they don't want to allow access. "That post got hit by lightning," I said to no one in particular.

"What?" someone said. A young man standing at the next pump was looking at me. I pointed. "That metal post over there by the school," I said. "It got hit by lightning."

"Damned if you aren't right about that," he said.

People were walking over and looking at the post, smiling and pointing and shaking their heads in disbelief. There was a flash in the sky. One-thousand-one, one-BaBoom! People ran from the post and slammed their car doors. I ducked inside the gas station. "What the hell was that?" asked the kid who took my money. "Lightning," I said breathlessly, "it struck that metal post at the school entrance."

"No shit?" the kid said. "That's totally awesome!"

"Yeah, awesome," I panted. I paid for my purchase quickly, then dashed for my truck and drove home. The lightning, it seemed, had spared me on the mountain at 7,000 feet elevation, only to follow me home and try to strike me at the bottom of the Kaweah River Canyon at less than 1000 feet! Stepping out of my muddy boots and clothes and leaving them in a heap at the back door, I was never so glad to close it tight behind me.

I latched the door behind me, as if that would help.

38

Trent And The Komatsu
In which we learn how not to break rocks!

Trent was breaking rocks with the Komatsu excavator and the whole crew was watching him. I'd been working for Milbro Construction, a Three Rivers company, for three summers building dry-laid rock walls in Sequoia National Park. The stone-setters I was working with were pretty good guys, people I knew from town and not such assholes as I normally dealt with on jobs. Doug Milton, the company owner, and Fritz with his long sweeping mustache, and Dean with his biker beard and long hair, and Ramananda the Hare Krishna, and Trent and the others, had become like a little family over the summers working together. We had our own man-camps on the sites and hung out around campfires in the evenings.

The walls we were building were big retaining walls for road cuts, parking lots, campgrounds and the new visitor facilities at the Wuksachi Village site. Constructed entirely of natural local granite with no concrete or mortar, the walls must stand strong, only the methods of their construction to give them integrity.

Some of the rocks coming out of the old Clover Creek Bridge quarry site were so massive that except for the first course on a new wall, that bottom section which is mostly buried as footings, they were too large to use. Much of the new stone was two or three times too big for any other purpose. A lot of time was being wasted on the jackhammers trying to crack them into smaller pieces. So Trent was using his huge machine.

He raised the arm of the excavator straight up, pointed the teeth of the bucket downwards and slammed the rock with the teeth. The sound of steel striking stone and the roar of the equipment's motor were deafening. The air around the excavator filled with dust as the tracks rocked back and forth on the powdery Sierra soil and the exhaust poured forth from the stack into the pristine mountain air. Trent hit the stones repeatedly. Some of them broke, some did not. He tried another tactic. Picking up a boulder with the thumb-mechanism on the bucket, he raised it high over another rock and dropped it.

Swoosh-CRACK!

We all were watching him now. Sitting up in the cab of the machine, his hands on the sticks, he swung the cab, lowered the arm, peeled the thumb back and snatched up the boulder again. He dangled it over the rock he was trying to break and dropped it again. With his close-cropped hair, pilot-shades, square-jaw set in a determined grimace, Trent looked like Arnold Schwartzenegger in "Terminator."

He had taken off his trademark plaid flannel shirt and hung it on the peg inside the cab and, wearing a white T-shirt stretched over a well-muscled chest, I could see his Popeye forearms bulge. Trent was so tough, I called him The Man of Steel. He moved deftly, as if his machine was a part of his own body, swinging this way and that, picking up boulders and dropping them on other boulders.

Swoosh-CRACK! Swoosh-CRACK! Swoosh-CRACK!

And to our delight, some of the rocks were breaking.

The stone-setters were getting excited. There would be fresh meat for the next wall. Already Fritz and Dean were scanning the new selections, planning to pounce on them as soon as it was safe. Ready to claim them, have them brought to their work area and make them part of their stable of personal stones.

There's a good one, look at those clean angles!

Oh, man, I gotta get my hands on that one!

The face on that one already has the right batter on it! Just pop it in and she's done!

And that one, shaped like the wing of a bird, that'll look awesome laid over a matching stone!

Trent's eyes behind the mirrored shades cast about. He spotted a big rock that wanted breaking. He picked up his best boulder and began tracking over. This is going to be good. Everyone stopped what they are doing to watch this. Trent toed the machine towards his victim, raising the boulder high in the air as he is still moving forward. A mud puddle was just ahead of him, a broad deep pool churned to a smooth chocolate milkshake by the huge tires and metal tracks of heavy equipment. Its slick glossy surface beckoned mischievously as Trent approached, his huge boulder dangling from his bucket. The arm rocked slightly back and forth as the machine lurched along, then the boulder wiggled free and fell.

FALOOOMP! The boulder made a perfect belly-flop into the mud puddle and a wave of milk chocolate mud rolled over Trent and the Komatsu.

I saw it all as if in slow motion. Trent, his Terminator face unflinching, the wall of mud striking him, covering every inch of his white T-shirt, his jeans, his work boots, his naked arms with the bulging muscles, his face. The mud coated the interior of the cab, the floor, the windowed sides, the plush seat, the hanging plaid shirt, Trent's lunch box tucked in the corner.

The machine lurched to a squealing halt.

The stone-setters were laughing, holding their bellies, doubled over. I was laughing so hard I feared I'd wet myself. I tried to stifle it, for Trent's sake. The Man of Steel was unmoving, his mud-covered self frozen in a tableau, like a statue carved out of a block of brown marble. We all stopped laughing and stood catching our breath, watching him.

Oh God, that was so funny!

Slowly, oh so slowly, Trent's hands released the joysticks and rose inch by inch to his face, globules of mud falling from his arms. Sedately, he removed his shades. His eyes were revealed in their raccoon-mask of white skin. He stared straight ahead for a moment, then furrowed his brow and looked down at himself, as if noticing for the first time that he had taken a mud bath.

We all went dead silent. Waiting for the punch line. Nothing was heard but the kitty-cat purr of the Komatsu's idling motor.

Then the Man of Steel spoke, loud enough for us all to hear.

"Well," he said, "this kind of breaks up the routine."

39

The Rock Dance
In which I seek the perfect stone

I shove my work gloves into a back pocket and unclip my tape measure from my belt. Zipping it out, I measure along the top of the empty space in the stone wall, then down from the top of the space to the bottom, then a couple quick measurements of other pertinent features of the space, a triangular gap between two stones near the lowest part of the hole, the depth of the hole from the string-line that marks the face of the wall to the large ugly boulder that sits in the backfill. Finally I step back and fix the shape of the space in my mind, picturing the rock that will fit there.

I trip across the rock pile in my scuffed work boots, the heavy nylon strap slung over my shoulders, its rough edge zinging against the soft skin of my neck above my collar. Jumping from rock to rock, laying my measure across several which are close in size or similar in shape to my space, I dance the dance of the stone-setter. Mostly it's an exercise, testing my eye, because I know that none of them are the rock I seek.

The rocks are loosely spread about, some of them jumbled together in heaps, some of them half-buried in the dirt what was scooped up with them when they were loaded into a dump-truck before being brought here.

I talk to them as I go, "Where are you from?" Deep within the earth, pushed to the light of day in some ancient upheaval. Blasted into the air by a road-builder's dynamite. Rolled a thousand miles by a glacier. "How old are you?" As old as the earth, as young as a dream, you pick because time means nothing to us. "Where in my wall do you want to be, or not at all?" A wall is a pile of rocks, not much different than the one we're in, except to you. Put us where you want, it is all the same. Break us, shape us, lever and lower us in, we'll bide there awhile. It's only a while, a hundred years or more, it is mere moments to us. If it gives you pleasure, we'll bide.

And there it is, the rock I seek. It looks nothing like the shape in my wall, at least not in its present posture. I get down on one knee and wedge myself between two bigger boulders, turning my head sideways and looking up at the underside of the rock where it had landed when tumbling out of the truck-bed. For fun I lay my measure on it this way and that way. Yes, it is the one.

I signal for my equipment operator. While he and his machine make their noisy way to me, I poke my strap under and around the rock, dirt falling into the cuffs of my gloves. I take them off and dump the dirt out of them, shaking them and then putting them back on. I snug the strap around the rock, running one loop through the other and adjusting for the hang I want. I rise from my knees and slap the dirt from my ragged jeans.

The operator sets up and swings his huge steel bucket towards me. I secure the strap to the iron hook and give a nod. Slowly, with a growl of engine and a squeal of metal, he raises the arm of the machine. The strap lifts, goes taut and begins to move the rock. It gives a grinding groan, emits a puff of dust and shifts, rolling about and assuming the upright posture I have strapped it for. It rises from its cradle in the boulders, swings slightly, turning in the air.

The face it presents to me is the one I had seen when on my knee with my head upside-down. It hangs suspended, its face battered precisely as it will sit in the wall. I am pleased with my selection. It is a choice made by the experienced eye of a stone-setter who has fitted many stones into many spaces, as with a three-dimensional jigsaw puzzle, and learned to recognize the sizes and shapes that will accommodate with an economy of energy expended. Hours, days, weeks, months and long summers at the jackhammer and the chipping gun have taught me to train my perceptions to see the shapes and sizes even when the stones are only half-visible.

It is almost an instinct, or perhaps it is what it feels like sometimes, a communication between oneself and the rocks. "Do you like that? Now we'll swing you into the wall."

It's as good as any. A new perspective, a place to bide. It might be fun, being part of a human construct for a while. Time will tell.

The backhoe bucket lowers the stone over the space in the wall. I guide it with one hand while signaling the operator with the other. It is hanging from its strap perfectly and lowers smoothly, bumping gently off the rock on one side then the other as, with a whisper of rubbing granite and a quiet thunk, it settles into place.

I continue twirling my finger downward and the strap slackens. I reach up and unhook the strap from the hook, flick my fingers outward to signal the operator that I'm clear. He swings the arm of the machine away, curls the bucket against the arm with a Clang!, raises the outriggers, turns his seat and rumbles off in a cloud of dust and diesel fumes to assist another stone-setter. Turning to my stone, I slip the strap through its loop and begin to wiggle it free from under the rock.

Using the end of my crowbar, I lift and tip my rock, and wiggle my strap, pulling gently until it pulls free in my hand. I make a few fine adjustments to the rock with the crowbar, reaching behind and under the rock to place a few chinkers to hold it in place, then begin the serious business of backfilling it, packing every void under, behind and around it with dirt and rubble, locking the stone in position.

When I am done, I stand back and admire, slapping the dirt from my clothing with my gloves. The stone looks like it belongs there, as if it is happy to bide there a hundred years or two, a stone's blink of an eye, while human babies grow up, grow old and die, and the people who built the wall are all forgotten.

I sigh at the profundity of it and my gaze falls on another space that wants filling. My hand flies to my tape measure and I click it off and zip it out, gauging the next empty space. There is a stone for this spot and I must find it.

Most think of stone as hard, cold and unyielding. But a stone-worker knows better. Every rock is different and even granite has variations. I've worked with solid white Sierra granite which, with tenacity and a lot of chipping, you could shape to almost anything. I've worked with tight-grained brittle blue Georgian granite which had a distinct grain to it and would shatter if you worked it without due diligence. I dealt with crumbling brown old granite, which you could carve like butter if you couldn't find a better rock to use. I encountered dark granite with huge gleaming black crystals, green granite with white veins of marble running through it, pink granite that you could split on a seam to discover rose quartz and butterfly both pieces into the wall.

Work with stone long enough and you begin to get a sense of where it wants to crack, how to avoid it cracking where you don't want it to and how to coerce it into playing your game.

The fact is, stone isn't cold and it isn't unyielding. It is as warm as the sunlight that streams down upon it, it holds the heat from that sunlight all day and well into the coldest night, and if you take the time to feel it, it radiates the warmth which emanates all the way from the core of the earth. It is yielding to the stone mason's concept. In most cases. There are rocks that simply will not play. They can never be made to hang in the strap with the proper batter to be lowered into the wall or they will roll right out of the strap no matter how carefully you strap them. They won't fit no matter how much a person chips on them, or once set, they'll fall right out of the wall the minute you turn your back to grab some backfill material. Some of them have been tried several different times by different stone-setters in different places and each time refused to participate.

"This one doesn't want to play rock wall," someone will holler and the operator will push it off to the side.

Ultimately, these rocks get used as backfill or saved for rip-rap in the creek-bed or simply cast off into the woods to pursue their own destiny. And rocks do have their own destiny, we can only divert their course for a little while.

Working with stone always gave me the feeling that I was participating in something timeless. Even if I wasn't going to be around long, the stone walls would be and the stones within them would remember the strike of my hammer and the touch of my hands.

like a fleeting caress on the face of the world.

Amy R Farrell

40

Mother And Son

In which my mother makes a promise

a, I think I'm fixing to die," my brother said over the phone line.

"Ah, honey," my mother said, anguish in her voice. She knew her son well enough to know he only used that Country Joe McDonald voice when things were really bad. Recently when he had spoken to her about death, he had asked that she be with him when he died, as she had been when he was born. She had told him that whenever he asked her, she would leave her house in West Marin and come stay with him in his San Francisco apartment. Hold him as she had when he was her "golden boy," the child with the flaming red hair and the bright blue eyes. See him from the world she had brought him into.

"The doc has just left," Steve went on, "and he said it ain't good."

My mother swallowed hard, trying to control the waver in her voice. "Do you want me to come now?"

She heard Steve take a ragged breath. "Well, not this minute. I mean... Doc said I may have a week or two. But soon."

"I have an awards ceremony tonight," my mother said. "They're giving me the Trudy Baum award for Community Service in Mental Health."

"That's terrific, Mom," Steve rasped, his voice barely a whisper.

"For the Creative Living Center," she added, something to say while she wiped the hot tears from her cheeks.

"Yes, I know, that's wonderful. You deserve it. So much." He paused, catching his breath. The pneumonia brought on by the sedentary nature of his long illness had made it increasingly hard to breathe. "What time is the ceremony?"

"I'm leaving here at five. There's a dinner after but I don't need to stay for that. But I don't need to go at all if--"

"You go, Ma. Get your award."

She choked back a sob. "I'll come right after."

"All right," he said. "I love you."

"I love you, too."

41

Pomp And Its Circumstance
In which reality is worse than worst imaginings

My mother attended the event, was feted, praised and cheered by her peers. She received her award and made her brief and humble acceptance speech. All the while, she hid her grief and anxiety from her friends, former clients and colleagues, all of whom wanted to share a moment or two with her, compliment her, congratulate her and reminisce with her over the years they had spent together at the Creative Living Center.

Steve was in her mind the entire evening as she talked, listened, shook hands, gave and received hugs, laughs and smiles. She excused herself before the dinner began and made her way to her car in the parking lot. Some friends followed her out to share a final few minutes with her, not knowing that she had somewhere urgent to go to, that she had a son dying with whom she had promised to be. My mother was never one for disappointing anyone and so she stayed another twenty minutes, giving of her time to the people who wanted to share it with her.   After all, Steve wanted her to enjoy this evening.

He had told her so.

Finally, alone in her car, she drove across the Golden Gate Bridge, her ears still ringing with the laughter, chatter, stories and applause of the evening, her mind filled with the faces of people who had been integral to the past twenty years of her life. Her face ached with all the smiling she had done and yet there was grief lodged like an acorn in her throat. It was a bittersweet mix of feelings, the warmth and fellowship she had just left and the destination to which she was heading, the quiet apartment where her son lay dying, awaiting her comfort and her presence.

She pictured the somber elegance of Steve's apartment where he lived with his partner Christian, in a beautiful old Victorian on California Street. The off-white walls of the high-ceilinged rooms, the dark hardwood furnishings, the sparse Zen-like ambiance. The room with the mullioned windows beyond which jasmine coiled up the outside wall and dangled just there, visible from Steve's huge cherry-wood bed. The tiny sunlit kitchen in the rear opening onto a small garden expertly designed and tended by Christian who made his living doing just that. The little bench among the wildly exuberant foliage in that garden, the bench Steve had not the strength to walk to, hadn't had for weeks.

She will find a parking space on one of the sharply-slanting streets in the neighborhood, parallel-park her Acura and walk along the dark sidewalks to the steps of his house. Mounting the staircase, she will ring the bell and Christian will open to her. In her mind she can see the clean lines of his face, the dark bangs cropped straight across his brow, his soulful eyes peering out from his wire-rimmed glasses. His full lips will purse slightly, sadly, and he will embrace his lover's mother, welcoming her into their home.

Silently, he will take her bag and precede her down the narrow hallway, setting the bag in the nook beside Steve's racing ten-speed where it stands gathering dust, many months unridden. The apartment will be still and peaceful, perhaps with the tones of Enya playing somewhere softly, beautifully. Candles will be burning in candleholders on the bureau as she enters Steve's room and his skeletal form will lay upon the great bed, covered with a cream-colored comforter.

"Stevie?" Christian will whisper. "Your mother is here."

The form under the comforter will shift: the head will turn; the hair on the pillow disheveled but still red-gold; the handsome cheeks now sunken and hollow, just skin stretched over bone; the huge blue eyes will meet hers.

There will be tears in those eyes, as there are in hers, but her son will smile and she will go to him.

Amy R Farrell

42

An Affinity For Stone
In which I touch something enduring and eternal

I'm almost at the top of the wall now. I've been working on this wall for two months and it is almost complete. Just a few more spaces along the top-line, one which looks like the state of Nebraska, one which is kind of an inverted isosceles triangle and one which must be long and flat but broad enough and heavy enough not to be pushed from the top by time, the elements or vandals.

I dance my dance, find three stones I think will make the grade and have them brought over to my rubble-strewn work area. Fixing my goggles over my eyes and clamping my hard hat tighter on my head, I pick up my chipping gun and begin knocking nubbins off the bearing surface of Nebraska. The gun jumps in my hands, frosty air blasting out of its port. Brrrapp! Brrrapp! Chips of granite fly from under the chisel-shaped bit. I score a line where I want the rock to crack and keep working it.   A nubbin breaks free.   Perfect!   I throw my leg over Nebraska and begin working on another nubbin.

Soon its ready and I set my gun down, lever one end of the rock up with my crowbar, prop it on a chinker and fish my strap under it. Fastening the strap, I slide it back and forth round the rock, gauging the weight and estimating the hang. Satisfied, I stand up and glance around to catch the attention of an operator. Trent spots me and spins the cab of his Komatsu, the big steel tracks squealing loudly as he tracks towards me.   He gently lowers the three-foot-wide bucket towards me and I reach up and hook my strap onto it.

I climb up the wall and lie in the backfill as Trent lowers the Nebraska rock slowly. This is where you have to be able to trust your operator. One false move and you are squashed. But Trent is one of the best I'd ever seen. As he lowers my rock, I stick my head down in the dirt and rubble to see how it will set. I need at least three-point contact for the rock to set solidly and it looks as if a boulder in the backfill is going to hang it up, causing a pivot point for the stone to tip from side to side. I shoot my arm straight up and close my fist, stopping Trent from lowering the stone. Sitting up in the backfill, I flick my fingers at him and hear the tone of the hydraulics change as he raises the stone and swings it safely away from me.   I drape my leg off the wall and scramble down.

Chipping gun in hand, I flip the hoses over the piles of rubble to give myself some slack. Jamming the steel-clad toe of one work boot into a crevasse in the wall-face, I begin to climb the stones. I chuck my gun up into the hole where the Nebraska rock will set, and make sure my feet were securely wedged in the wall before I grab the gun and begin chipping the boulder in the backfill that needs modification. Brrrapp! Brrrapp! Brrrapp! Chips of granite ping off my goggles and sting my face.

The smell of chipped granite tweaks my sinuses, the ozone smell of tiny lightning strikes. I stop and pull my bandana up to cover my mouth and nose. This helps a little but soon my goggles begin to fog up and I pull the bandana down. My calves are in spasm from clinging by my toes to the rock wall. My quads are burning like I have just done thirty leg-presses, but I keep chipping the boulder, feeling the cramping in my hands and my trigger finger turning ice cold, feeling the bunching of my shoulder muscles and the flexing of my biceps, the hardness of my forearm.

I press hard, leaning into the gun where its steel bit jounces and beats on the rock, skipping around until I redouble my efforts to hold it in one place. Bits fly from the steel and little sparks dance out into the air, one of them burning my face. Crack! The rock breaks and I release the trigger. Whew! I drop the gun in the granite dust, dirt and rubble of the backfill and pick up the piece I just chipped off, chucking it to the side in case I need it for a chinker when I set the stone. My hands tingle, the nerves sending little jolts to my fingertips. I lower the gun down to the ground by its hose and clamber down after it.

With a nod at Trent, he and I set the stone.

It settles into its space in the top-line as if it had waited all its long existence for just this moment in time.

43

Shadow Chaser
In which my mother races time

My mother drives down a dark street. It is an October night in San Francisco and a light mist hangs between the Victorian houses. A few cars pass, headlights flaring in her eyes, here and there dark forms stroll on dark sidewalks. She is watching each street-name sign, looking for Steve's street. It is somewhere just up ahead. She hopes it is easy to find a space, she doesn't want to have to walk far carrying her overnight bag and her handbag over her shoulder. It is a pretty safe neighborhood, but still, it is already quite dark. The street lamps are lit and insects spiral about each other in the glow.

She is anxious to arrive, has had to be careful to avoid speeding, yet she is also terrified. How is she to do this? She has done a lot of things for a lot of people, this evening was a celebration of all that she has done, but how does she help her son to die? Her heart is racing and her mouth is cotton. There are gritty tears dried on her cheeks. She takes one hand from the wheel and rubs at her face, works her tongue around in her mouth to get the saliva going, and practices her smile. It will be better once she gets there. Once she is there, with Steve, she will know what to do. God, Steve. Her eyes sting with fresh tears, blurring her vision. She wipes them away with the back of her hand.

Right now she has to pull herself together. She has to be strong, for Christian, who will open the door and let her in. For Steve, who waits for her to come. She is here for them. She is here to do whatever Steve needs. She is here to love him, hold him, listen to him, help him through this.

There will be time for herself, after.

In her rearview mirror a flashing red light blossoms, a siren rips the night. She pulls carefully to the side and allows the ambulance to pass, then falls in behind it. It pulls away, outdistancing her quickly. A sudden dread clutches her by the throat. Oh my God, don't let it turn on California street! Unconsciously, my mother's foot presses the gas and she accelerates, keeping her eye on the flashing light. Somewhere up ahead, it turns, winking out of sight.

Oh, no. Oh, Steve. My mother presses down on the pedal, passes one intersection, not California, passes another, not California, reaches a third, California, slows for the turn and brings the car around it. The ambulance in full flash is double-parked several houses down. In front of Steve and Christian's house. My mother's heart lodges in her throat.

She pulls the Acura in right behind the ambulance, slams it into park, and leaps out. The flashing lights cause her shadow, her multiple shadows, to gandy-dance across the broken concrete sidewalk.

She chases her shadows to Steve's stairs.

44

Remember Me

In which I ask a favor of Earth

I lie on my belly on top of the wall. Using my gloved hand as a trowel, I push dirt down through gaps between the stones. Fine dust curls up like little smoke-signals into my nostrils as the dirt filters down into the interior of the wall.

A tendril of hair which has worked its way free from my braid falls across my face, tickling me. I flip off a glove and with a dirty forefinger push the hair back behind my ear. I move my head and align my eye with face of the wall.

Looking down from the lip to the base, I admire the perfectly consistent batter I have achieved with the aid of the string line. Turning my head, I sweep my gaze over the wall from here to the end. The wall goes straight as an arrow for a hundred feet, then comes to a perfect right angle at an inside corner, then executes a sweeping radius before diving down into the ground and disappearing, all while maintaining the same angle of repose. It is a thing of beauty.

Examining it now, on my belly in the dirt, I marvel that such a thing can be built out of rough odd shapes of native stone, hacked and hewn with tools as imprecise as a jackhammer, held in place with nothing but their own weight and balance, mortared together with nothing more adherent than dry dirt and rock chips.

And yet, they'll stand the test of time. How long? I don't know. I won't be here to see when this wall comes tumbling down.

With my ungloved hand, I touch the rock I lay upon. I close my eyes for a moment and feel its warmth, its solidity under my palm. Its strength, its patience and its purpose. My fingertips stroke its rough surface.

Granite. Bones of Mother Earth. What an honor to have worked with you.

You'll carry on, won't you? When I am gone?

You'll remember? If not me, then at least my kind?

44

A Kite In The Storm
In which my brother flies away

The front door is ajar.

My mother races down the hallway, slides to a stop at the door to Steve's bedroom. Three paramedics and their kits fill the room. Their bright white uniforms and gleaming equipment seem an invasion into this peaceful chapel of a space. Indeed, my mother notices, a candle burns in its sconce on the bureau and the soaring notes of R. Carlos Nakai's flute rise and fall over the voices of the medical professionals.

"Does this man have AIDS?" one man queries.

"Yes," Christian cries. He is on the bed, holding Steve by the shoulders. One medic is also on the bed, giving chest compressions so hard the frail body bounces up and down. Another medic places a plastic devise in Steve's slack mouth and begins delivering air. A third medic, kneeling at bedside, snaps open a hard case and begins preparing something my mother can't see. Christian calls Steve's name in a voice filled with panic.

My mother leaves her body and floats above the scene, looking down. The big cream-colored bed, crowded with persons. The uniformed men whose ministrations seem a desecration. Christian, his strong healthy body wracked with sobs. The body of her son, wizened to nothing and empty now. Herself in the doorway, shoulder against the jamb, one hand over her mouth.

*   *   *

On a windy storm-threatening day on the shoulder of Mount Tamalpais, a crowd of nearly a hundred gather to remember Steve Farrell. They range in age from infant to eighties, and come from all places in life. Blankets spread in a mountain meadow, wet grass quickly soaking though wool, warm jackets and hats pulled tight against the chill, they sit or stand flanked by fir trees whose tops thrash against a darkening sky.

In the center of the circle, my cowboy hat held on my head by a hurricane strap lashed under my chin, I beat the drum and chant a Native American prayer. I am filling a role traditional in my family, that of priest, though of a different nature than the Catholic one intended for my father. In the distance, my brother Peter, the black sheep of the family, his samurai face fixed against sorrow, honors Steve in the only way he knows how, flying a massive dragon kite in the turbulent sky, fighting the pull of the wind as the colorful kite battles against the strings which hold it.

When my drum falls silent, people speak. They share what they know and love about Steve. His boss tells the story of Steve developing a chip that had caused a sea-change in computer engineering. He tells how the company had decided to etch his name in microscopic script on every chip that came off the production line as a testament to my brother's talent. Who knows, the man says, how far Steve would have gone in his field if he had lived. "Amazing for a man who never completed college, a natural genius," he concluded.

Others speak of Steve's friendship, his heart, his boyish good humor and his fun. Some reveal what a tiger he was when mounted on a racing bicycle, how he powered up mountains like nobody's business and ate up the miles in an all-out race. What speed and stamina and grace he had when his feet were in the pedal-clips.

Some recount his love of nature, long hikes and camping trips in canyons, on beaches and in wilderness. His wild exuberance on roller-skates in Golden Gate Park on a Sunday afternoon. How he rode a Norton motorcycle up the California coast back in the seventies all the way to Oregon.

They spoke of his ability to fix anything from MG sports cars to fine electronics. Some tell how he had helped them endure the loss of their own loved ones to AIDS. Each story reveals a man who gave much to his friends and shared with them his love affair with life. People weep openly as they tell of the friend they knew. People weep openly as they listen.

My own family's faces tell how deep this grief runs. Jody's tale of her twenty minutes talking in the parking lot after the Trudy Baum award ceremony repeats itself in my mind. Her remorse that those precious minutes squandered robbed her and her son of their final connection.

This possibility is a deep abiding sorrow that will hold my mother forever in its grip.

I look up at the sky, the damp fog blowing hard across the ridge, the treetops lashing to and fro, Peter's kite nearly lost in the flailing mist.

The cold and damp are deepening, soon this gathering must break up. I cast my eyes over the faces of these people who loved my brother. It hits me, suddenly, that Steve would have spared them all this grief if he could have. He could suffer the agony of his disease with the stoicism that was his nature, but his heart would break if he could see what his passing had done to us all. And like a revelation, I know why he died while my mother was on her way to him. Why he had died right then, that very night, the night he had asked her to come stay with him until the end.

In his heart of hearts, he knew this his last chance to spare her the pain of witnessing his death. As much as he wished for the comfort of her presence in his final hours, he wanted to spare her that.

He was his mother's son.

I raise my head against the stinging wind and look up into the wild sky, just in time to see Peter's kite break its string and sail off into the mist.

Its bright colors fade into the swirling gray.

45

Visitation

In which I am reminded of my brother's legacy to me

I come awake suddenly as if someone has given me a hard shake. "Steve?" I cry but only silence answers. My eyes have sprung open but I am staring into darkness. Where am I? I grope about me, feel the wall, the edge of the narrow bed, the cracked linoleum floor. The trailer! I am in the trailer on the mountain, in the man-camp. Off on the very edge of the man-camp in the dark forest near the creek. Where I went to bed last night feeling sad and alone because my brother was dead. Where I had lain awake long tremulous hours thinking every sound was a visitation. Wanting one. Fearing one.

But why do I feel he was just with me, just now, just <u>this</u> close?

Then I remember the dream. It comes back clear and sharp. I am sitting with Steve on the broad white marble steps of City Hall. Reclining at ease on the step above mine, my brother is backlit by a warm sun, his red hair aglow, mustache trim and neat. He is wearing designer jeans and expensive sneakers. His arms exposed by the muscle-shirt he wears are tanned and strong, his torso lean and limber, and his face is joyous. He listens I tell him all about doing the rock work in Sequoia, the beautiful walls I'm so proud to be building, the walls which will last for hundreds of years. The dance of stone-setting.

"I'd like to show them to you some time. I think you'd really dig them!"

Steve's eyes are a vibrant blue in the sunlight. "I'd like to see them," he says. "I'm sure I will. They will be there a very, very long time."

I smile, remembering him in the 70's when he was a hippy farmer living in the woods of Oregon, when his red hair was long and wind-tangled down his back and his beard was full and bushy, like a copper-colored thicket. I remember when I visited his farmhouse when I was thirteen and spent a week helping him cut and stack pine logs for the wood stove. He ran the greasy old chainsaw and I helped split logs with a maul. He wore a Pendleton shirt and Levis 501s and work boots with steel toes. He seemed like a different man then, an earthy mountain man as opposed to the city-slicker he is now, the computer genius and man of the future. Either way, he is still my brother and I am proud.

"I love you, bro," I say.

"I love you too," Steve says.

People are climbing and descending the stairs on either side of us in business clothes and carrying briefcases, some, like us, in jeans and T-shirts. A black man playing a conga drum is at the top of the steps. Passersby drop dollar bills in his hat. Pigeons peck for crumbs and cars pass on the street in front of us. We sit and share the moment, enjoying the sun and the San Francisco day.

Steve leans forward to kiss my cheek. His trim mustache tickles. "Well, Sis, I have to get going." He glances up and smiles at a couple walking up the stairs past us.

"Going?" I say. "But I just got here. Can't we talk a little longer?"

His eyes meet mine. "It's been great seeing you but you've got to be getting back. And I have work to do." He jumps to his feet and pulls me up after. I sigh and hug him hard.

Trying to hold him a moment longer and admittedly curious, I ask, "What kind of work are you doing?" People are streaming up and down the steps. This is a very busy place! Steve nods and smiles at a woman going by before he turns back to me. His smile is as blinding as the sunlight striking the white marble. He is so handsome, and so smart, and so sweet, and he is <u>my</u> brother!

"I have to help other people," he says. "You know, other people who just got here."

"Help them do what?" I ask.

Steve smiles at another passerby and looks at me. "Help them find their way. Until they know what they are going to do next."

He turns and bounds up three or four steps.

Pivoting on one sneakered foot, my brother looks down at me. "Oh, and Sis..."

As I look up at him, the sun streaks into my eye, bringing a tear. "What?"

"Remember, don't wait for life."

He smiles, then bounds like a gazelle up the stairs.

Amy R Farrell

46

A Place To Be

In which I'll stop to muse awhile

Just days ago I drove up the winding mountain road from my home and took the General's Highway into Sequoia National Park to pay a visit to the stone walls of Wuksachi Village. They still stand stoically, a testament to our labor and our lives. An hour later, I walked the Soldier's Trail, searching for my old friend, The Flaming Arrow, in the heart of the Giant Forest. I had not been there since the day in 1985 when Trey and I stood watching the tree burn. I feared what I might find, but to my relief and joy, I found a still-living tree. But rather than just the single hole in the tree's side and a hollowed-out interior, I found a half tree. From forest floor to sky, one half of the giant is completely burned-away. The half that stands has living limbs and foliage high up. Not the healthiest example of a Giant Sequoia, but at least still alive. Further down the trail, John Muir's Broken Arrow is exactly as I remember it. On the Congress Trail near the General Sherman Tree, I was shocked to find that the Spyglass Tree had toppled since my last visit. A tangle of bark, charred wood, shattered limbs and brown foliage is all that remains. Thus, even the ancient trees are in a state of change.

I still wish that my brother Steve had seen the stone walls. I wish my father had heard me tell of The Flaming Arrow, and lived, as a healthy man with a good heart, to walk the trails of the Giant Forest and see the tree sculptures. Maybe in a way, they have. For I know, at least intellectually, that all things are connected, past, present, and future, and that there is no separation between me and all living beings and the objects of the earth and the bodies of the universe and the energies, seen and unseen, with which we come into contact. I know that our perceptions of our world and our lives are but a construct of our minds, an attempt to make sense of the enormity of existence. Do the bones of the earth and the great trees even notice us? And does it matter? Or does it only matter that we be here with them in our time?

I always have had an affinity for wood and stone.

Once when I was a child I skipped school and tied myself to a tree in our back yard to defend it from being cut down. The neighbors objected to the leaves and nuts it dropped on their side. It was not the tree's fault, I reasoned, that the neighbors didn't know a good thing when it fell over their fence.

As for rocks, I collected so many in cardboard egg cartons that a family friend, Noa Bornstein, hand-painted a "box for rocks" of my very own, adorned with a yellow-haired freckle-faced girl (me) and the words, "I think this is a friendly box. This can be a box for rocks (or smiles)" and "I like mice" with a picture of a girl with hundreds of little multicolored mice climbing into her lap. Moon and stars, a field of flowers, my box for rocks was a pretty piece of work.

Wood and stone have kept me company all my life. At age fifty-four, I find myself living in a house made of wood and stone, built upon a rock outcropping in the shade of pines and oaks, with a view to the east of a great granite dome known as Big Baldy in the Sequoia National Forest. Living here with me, besides a wonderful woman, are critters of many kinds, mostly rescued from shelters, slaughterhouses and roadsides. They are my friends and my family.

Human beings are always building. Made in the image of the Creator, we are always mimicking that creative impulse. These things we build to shelter our families, to conduct our business, to facilitate our movement as human beings wild and free on the planet, these things made mostly of wood and stone, they are a legacy. They last long after the hands that made them are gone. My brother's computer chip. The parks and buildings my father designed, the artful towers he helped save. My mother's creative living that improved the lives of so many, her tender parenting that taught her children how to parent their own children. My roads and bridges, my stone walls, these things last long after the flesh has gone to dust. Maybe as long as the great trees of the Sierras.

In my life as a construction worker, wood and stone have, in one way or another, been my livelihood since I was seventeen. Wood and stone are not just the medium of my work, they have been my partners in it. We work together. This notion appeals to me because, in many ways, I had to be a rock to do this work. As well, I had to be wood, bendable and flexible and tough, for I had entered into a maze-like subculture where women rarely tread. The stories of my adventures in No Woman's Land are the stories of wood and stone and me.

My father, the Ecstatic Dancer, said I should give my stories to the world. Well, here is one, offered in case anyone cares to read it.

More will follow.

After all, we all have a story. We all leave a past, a story, something, behind.

Some of what we leave is tangible, some is not. Some is as ethereal as memories, as powerful and elusive as love.

THE END

About The Author

Amy R Farrell lives in the Sierra Foothills
near Sequoia National Park with her life partner and their
horses, dogs, cats and birds. She is a practicing natural
barehoof trimmer of equines and supervises work
crews for the Public Works Department of the
County of Tulare, California.

If you enjoyed this book, check out Amy's second memoir,
Adventures In No Woman's Land,
More War Stories of a Female Construction Worker,
coming in spring of 2014.

To view photos relating to this book, visit
www.armsmerepress.com

Made in the USA
San Bernardino, CA
29 November 2013